BIG CAT

THE ST. CROIX COUGAR

J. D. BEAUFEAUX

Order this book online at www.trafford.com
or email orders@trafford.com

Most Trafford titles are also available at major online book retailers.

Printed in the United States of America.

ISBN: 978-1-4669-3034-6 (sc)
ISBN: 978-1-4669-3036-0 (hc)
ISBN: 978-1-4669-3035-3 (e)

Library of Congress Control Number: 2012907678

Trafford rev. 06/04/2012

   www.trafford.com

North America & international
toll-free: 1 888 232 4444 (USA & Canada)
phone: 250 383 6864 ♦ fax: 812 355 4082

THIS BOOK HAS TAKEN OVER THREE YEARS OF RESEARCH AND DEDICATION TO WRITE. I WANT TO SHOWN MY GRATITUDE AND APPRECIATION TO MY FRIEND, SANDY WHO NOT ONLY WAITED PATIENTLY FOR ME TO FINISH THE BOOK BUT ALSO, WAS A GREAT HELP WITH MY SPELLING AND THE USE OF HER COMPUTER.

ALTHOUGH IT IS A RECOGNIZED FACT THAT CHEETAHS, PANTHERS AND LEOPARDS HAVE BEEN RECORDED PULLING THEIR KILLS INTO TREES TO HIDE THEM FROM OTHER PREDATORS. IT IS NOT A GENERAL FACT THAT MOUNTAIN LIONS OR COUGARS DO THE SAME. HOWEVER; THE NORTH AMERICAN MOUNTAIN LION HAS THE STRENGTH AND THE ABILITY TO DO JUST THAT. FOR THE SAKE OF ENTERTAINMENT AND BECAUSE IT HAS NOT BEEN DISPROVEN THAT MOUNTAIN LIONS OR COUGARS *CAN'T* HIDE THERE KILLS IN A TREE THE AUTHOR CHOSE TO INCLUDE THIS POSSIBILITY IN THIS BOOK.

CHAPTER 1

AFTER THE FIRST CHASE

IT WAS A CLOUDY, COLD EVENING IN MARCH OF 2009 WHEN BIG CAT; A COUGAR, WALKED TO THE ENTRANCE OF HIS LAIR AND STRETCHED HIS LONG, MUSCULAR BODY AFTER A WEARY DAYS REST. CAREFULLY STEPPING OUT OF HIS DEN HIS EARS TWITCHED BACK AND FORTH LISTENING TO EVERY SOUND AS HIS NOSE CHECKED THE WIND FOR ANY SCENT OF DANGER. HE WAS STILL FEELING UNEASY FROM THE PREVIOUS DAYS ADVENTURE WHEN BAYING HOUNDS HAD CHASED HIM FOR MILES AND TREED HIM AFTER HE WAS EXHAUSTED FROM RUNNING FOR SO LONG.

THE ECHOING VOICES OF THOSE YAPPING HOUNDS IN HIS MIND AND THE MEN WHO CAME BEHIND THEM MADE HIS HAIR STAND UP ON THE BACK OF HIS NECK! HE RECALLED THE FEAR AND RAGE HE FELT AS HE SAT TRAPPED IN THE TREE WITH THE HOUNDS BARKING, LOUDLY AT HIM; PLUS THE MEN WITH THEIR LOUD FIRE-STICKS WHICH MADE HIM CRINGE AS HE RECALLED THE DEATH OF OTHER ANIMALS HE HAD SEEN KILLED BY THEM. AND FINALLY, THE RELIEF HE FELT WHEN THE DOGS WERE PULLED BACK ALLOWING HIM TO LEAP TO THE GROUND AND RACE AWAY.

HIS HUNGER BROUGHT HIM BACK TO THE PRESENT AS HE FELT HIS STOMACH GROAN FOR FOOD. IT HAD BEEN OVER TWO DAYS SINCE HE HAD EATEN FROM A DEER CARCASS; A WINTER KILL THAT HAD BEEN FROZEN AND PRESERVED. HOWEVER; THE DOGS HAD DRIVEN HIM MANY MILES FROM THE CARCASS SO HE HAD TO LOOK FOR OTHER FOOD SINCE HE HAD ONLY EATEN; LIGHTLY.

WALKING OUT OF HIS LAIR INTO THE OPEN; HE CHECKED THE AREA FOR ANY PREY. TO HIS RIGHT WAS A TAMARACK SWAMP WHICH USUALLY DIDN'T OFFER ANYTHING HE COULD EAT BUT ON THE LEFT WAS HIGHER GROUND WITH BIG OAK TREES AND HE SAW A SQUIRREL, SCURRY ACROSS THE FOREST FLOOR.

GENERALLY, HE DIDN'T BOTHER WITH SQUIRRELS BUT HIS HUNGER PAINS DROVE HIM FORWARD AND HE HAD TO TRY. IN A LOW, CROUCHING POSITION; HE SILENTLY CREPT TOWARDS THE SQUIRREL BUT BEFORE HE GOT CLOSE THE SQUIRREL SAW HIM AND HURRIED UP THE TREE TO THE TOP. BIG CAT KNEW THAT IT WAS USELESS TO TRY TO CLIMB AFTER THE SQUIRREL, SINCE IT COULD EASILY JUMP TO BRANCHES IN OTHER TREES AND ESCAPE HIM.

AS THE SKY DARKENS AND THE AIR MOISTENS; SOUNDS AND SCENTS ARE CARRIED FURTHER THAN DURING THE DAY. BIG CAT'S KEEN SENSE OF SMELL IS A VITAL PART OF HIS HUNTING ABILITIES AND WITH THE ODORS OF THE FOREST FILLING HIS NOSE WITH SCENTS LIKE FROGS, RACCOONS, WILD TURKEYS AND DEER; HE BEGINS TO SEARCH FOR FOOD. SCANNING THE AREA IN THE LOW LIGHT; HE COULD SEE CLEARLY THE DIFFERENCES BETWEEN TREES, BRUSH AND PREY BECAUSE LIKE ALL CATS AND SOME OTHER PREDATORS; THEIR IRIS'S OPEN VERTICAL AND CAN EXPAND TO THE *FULL WIDTH OF THE EYE* ALLOWING MORE LIGHT TO ENTER. THUS; THEY CAN SEE EVERYTHING MORE DISTINCTLY THEN *WE CAN* IN VERY *LITTLE LIGHT.*

COUGARS ALSO; HAVE LONG WHISKERS LIKE HOUSE CAT THAT WARNING THEM WHEN SOMETHING IS CLOSE TO THEIR FACE IN THE DARK AND WHEN THE WIND BLOWS ACROSS THEM THEY CAN SENSE THAT TOO! A CAT'S WHISKERS ARE VERY IMPORTANT TO THEM IN LOW–LIGHT BECAUSE WITH THEM THEY ARE ABLE TO "VIEW' THEIR SURROUNDINGS—*SO TO SPEAK*—BY FEELING ANY OBSTACLE THAT THEY MAY COME IN CONTACT WITH AS THEY SEARCH FOR FOOD IN DARK AREAS.

BIG CAT FOLLOWED THE STRONG, MUSKY SCENTS COMING FROM A NEARBY POND AND TRIED TO SNEAK UP ON SOME CROAKING FROGS. THE MARSHES EDGE SANK UNDER HIS FEET AND HE JUMPED BACK AS WATER GOT HIS FEET WET. HE TRIED ANOTHER APPROACH TO GET NEAR THE FROGS IN THE MARSH BUT AGAIN HE STARTED TO SINK NTO THE MARSH. SOMETHING MOVED TO HIS RIGHT AND HE SAW A TURTLE TRYING TO PADDLE AWAY BUT IT WAS SLOWED DOWN BY THE WEEDS AS IT STRUGGLED TO GET AWAY. HE BATTED WITH HIS PAW AT

THE TURTLE BUT ONLY SUCCEEDED IN SPLASHING WATER AS THE TURTLE SWAM AWAY.

AFTER TRYING ONCE MORE TO CATCH A FROG; BIG CAT DECIDED IT WASN'T WORTH GETTING WET OVER. TURNING AWAY FROM THE MARSH; HE LEFT HIS MARK BY RAISING HIS TAIL HIGH AND SQUIRTING ON A TREE LEAVING HIS SCENT TO MARK HIS BOUNDARIES; THEN WENT LOOKING FOR OTHER MEALS.

THE DNR (DEPARTMENT OF NATURAL RESOURCES) HAD RECEIVED A NUMBER OF PROFESSED SIGHTINGS FROM RESIDENTS CLAIMING TO SEE COUGARS OVER THE YEARS; ALSO KNOW AS A PUMAS, PANTHERS OR MOUNTAIN LIONS. MOST SIGHTINGS WERE FOUND TO BE OTHER ANIMALS; LIKE CANADIAN LYNX, BOBCATS, LARGE DOGS AND A VARIETY OF OTHER ANIMALS. HOWEVER; WITH THE MORE FREQUENT USE OF TRAIL CAMERAS, SPOTTING COUGARS HAS BECOME MUCH LESS DIFFICULT AND COUGARS HAVE BEEN RECORDED ON FILM.

CHAPTER 2

THE SECOND CHASE

ON THE MORNING OF THE FIRST SIGHTING OF BIG CAT; STEVE THOMPSON, A VETERAN MOUNTAIN LION HUNTER RECEIVED A CALL FROM A FRIEND THAT BELIEVED THERE WERE TRACKS OF A COUGAR ON HIS PROPERTY. WHEN STEVE ARRIVED; HE CHECKED OUT THE TRACKS AND AGREED THAT THEY WERE MOUNTAIN LION TRACKS . . . THAT WAS THE BEGINNING OF THE FIRST CHASE. THE DAY AFTER LETTING BIG CAT GO FROM THE TREE; STEVE WAS BACK WITH HIS DOGS WHEN THE DNR REQUESTED HIS HELP IN TRYING TO COLLAR THE CAT. WITH MODERN TECHNOLOGY COLLARING A WILD ANIMAL IS THE BEST WAY TO KEEP TRACK OF THE WHEREABOUTS OF THEE ANIMAL.

THE EARLY MORNING SUN CREATED ICE CRYSTALS THAT SPARKLED AND CREATED RAINBOWS OF LIGHT AROUND BELOW HIM AS BIG CAT RESTED IN A COMFORTABLE TREE DREAMING OF FAR AWAY PLACES. HIS DREAMS WERE DISTURBED AS THE SOUND OF DISTANT BAYING HOUNDS REACHED HIS EARS. IN HIS DROWSINESS; HE THOUGHT IT WAS JUST ANOTHER BAD DREAM BUT THE INCREASING VOLUME OF THE HOUNDS BROUGHT HIM FULLY AWAKE.

LISTENING CLOSELY; BIG CAT COULD TELL THAT THEY WERE COMING HIS WAY AND HE KNEW HE HAD TO RUN. HE QUICKLY CLIMBED DOWN FROM THE TREE AND BOUNDED STRAIGHT AWAY FROM THE THREAT. RUNNING AT A STEADY PACE HE NOTICED A FIELD WITH A FARM AHEAD OF HIM AND KNOWING THE DANGER OF MAN AND THE FEAR OF BEING IN THE OPEN IN DAYLIGHT; HE TURNED TOWARDS THE DENSER COVER TREES.

QUICKENING HIS PACE; HE LOPED AWAY FROM THE SOUND OF THE HOUNDS AND SURPRISED A DOE AND FAWN AS HE CAME OVER A HILL. THEY RACED AWAY AS BIG CAT RAN BY IGNORING THEM; KNOWING THAT HE HAD TO FLEE THE DOGS AND COULDN'T STOP TO HUNT. SHORTLY AFTER THAT; THE SCENT OF HUMAN'S AND THEIR LEFTOVER FOOD DUMPED OUTSIDE REACHED HIS NOSE AS HE PASSED CLOSE TO A HOUSE.

HE CONTINUED RUNNING AWAY FROM THE PURSUING HOUNDS IGNORING HIS HUNGER AS HE LOPPED ALONG. THE SNOW HAD BEGUN TO MELT AND AS HE RAN ALONG THE FOREST FLOOR IT WOULD ALTERNATE FROM BEING SNOW COVERED TO LEAFY SOFT GROUND.

AFTER RUNNING FOR A NUMBER OF MILES; BIG CATS FAST PACE WAS EXHAUSTING HIM SO HE SLOWED TO A WALK WHEN HE REALIZED THE HOUNDS BAYING HAD SLACKENED. STOPPING AND PANTING; HE REGAINED HIS BREATH AND LISTENED FOR THE BAYING HOUNDS HOPING THAT THE DOGS HAD STOPPED CHASING HIM.

FINDING A PINE TREE WITH LOW-HANGING BRANCHES, HE STEPPED UNDER THEM FOR SHELTER AND HE LAID DOWN TO REST FOR A MOMENT. HE HAD BARELY CAUGHT HIS BREATH WHEN HE HEARD THE SHARP BAYING OF THE LEAD DOG CLOSING IN ON HIM.

BIG CAT JUMPED TO HIS FEET AND RACED OFF IN BIG BOUNDS WITH HIS LONG TAIL SWAYING BEHIND HIM GIVING HIM BETTER BALANCE. VARIOUS SCENTS OF THE FOREST ENTERED HIS NOSE AS HE SPED ALONG JUMPING OVER FALLEN TREES AND DODGING THICK BRUSH AS HE CONTINUED ON HIS WAY.

AFTER TRAVELING FOR SOME TIME, THE SCENT OF A SKUNK STUNG HIS NOSE AND HE SWERVED TO STAY AWAY FROM THE ANIMAL IN HIS PATH. NOT LONG AFTER THAT THE PUNGENT ODOR OF TAR FILLED HIS NOSE AS HE BOUNDED ACROSS A PAVED ROAD. FORTUNATELY FOR HIM; THERE WEREN'T ANY CARS ON THE ROAD WHEN HE PASSED OVER IT. PASSING THROUGH THE WOODS; HE SAW A GROUP OF HOUSES AHEAD OF HIM AND HE TURNED TO THE DENSER TREES AWAY FROM THE HOMES FOR BETTER COVER.

HIS MUSCLES WERE STARTING TO ACHE AND HIS BREATHING GREW HEAVIER AS HE CONTINUED RUNNING WITH THE DOGS BAYING AND CLOSING IN ON HIM. BOUNDING BACK AND FORTH THROUGH THE THICK BRUSH AND LEAPING OVER FALLEN TREES SLOWED HIS PACE BUT BIG CAT KNEW FROM EXPERIENCE THAT

HE HAD TO CONTINUE RUNNING TO KEEP AHEAD OF THE PACK EVEN THOUGH HIS CHEST BEGAN TO HURT.

KNOWING THE DANGER THAT A PACK OF DOGS BROUGHT TO HIM AND THE HELPLESS FEELING OF BEING TREED BY THEM BROUGHT BACK A RISING ANGER IN BIG CAT. SEEING THAT THE LEAD DOG HAD RAN AHEAD OF THE OTHER HOUNDS; HE CROUCHED BEHIND A BIG OAK TREE AND WAITED TO ATTACK.

UNAWARE OF THE HIDDEN COUGAR; THE DOG CAME BOUNDING FORWARD DOWN THE PATH AND WHEN HE REACHED THE TREE; BIG CAT LEAPT FROM BEHIND IT AND SANK HIS TEETH INTO THE BACK OF THE DOG AS IT PASSED BY HIM. THE HOUND YELPED AND TWISTED HIS HEAD AROUND JUST ENOUGH TO NIP AT BIG CAT'S EAR. THE NIP ON HIS EAR SURPRISED BIG CAT AND HE LET THE DOG GO.

IN RESPONSE, THE DOG JUMPED AT BIG CAT BUT THE CAT RETALIATED SWINGING HIS POWERFUL FRONT PAW BARELY MISSING THE DODGING DOG AS HE PULLED AWAY. THE FIGHT CONTINUED WITH LOUD BARKING AND GROWLING AS THEY LUNGED BACK AND FORTH AT EACH OTHER. CATCHING THE DOG OFF GUARD; BIG CAT SAW HIS CHANCE AND WITH A QUICK SWING OF HIS RIGHT PAW HE SLASHED THE SIDE OF THE HOUND OPEN AS THE DOG HOWLED IN PAIN.

BY THAT TIME THE OTHER HOUNDS WERE CLOSING IN ON HIM; SO BIG CAT TURNED AND LEAPT HIGH UP THE TREE THAT HE HAD BEEN HIDING BEHIND JUST AS THE OTHER DOGS ARRIVED SNAPPING AT HIS TAIL. CLIMBING OUT ON A HIGH LIMB HE STARED DOWN AT THE BARKING DOGS AS THEY TRIED TO LEAP UP THE TREE AFTER HIM.

AFTER SOME TIME, BIG CAT HEARD MEN TALKING AND APPROACHING THROUGH THE TREES. AS THE MEN CONTINUED TO DRAW CLOSER HE SLUNK DOWN ON THE LIMB HOPING THE MEN WOULDN'T SEE HIM. HE SAW THE MEN RESTRAIN THERE DOGS AS HE FOUGHT THE DESIRE TO JUMP AND RUN. HE SNARLED DOWN AT THE MEN AS THEY HELD THE DOGS BACK; CLIMBING FURTHER OUT ON THE LIMB IN AN FUTAL ATTEMPT TO ESCAPE THE MEN RIGHT UNDER HIM.

ONE OF THE MEN AIMED A FIRE-STICK AT HIM AND THE EXPLOSION STARTLED BIG CAT AS A PIECE OF BARK FLEW FROM THE BRANCH NEXT TO HIM AND HE GROWLED DOWN AT HIS CAPTORS.

THEN HIS INSTINCT FOR SURVIVAL OVER-CAME HIS FEAR AND HE REACTED; TURNING AWAY FROM THE MEN AND DOGS, BIG CAT LEAPT AS HARD AS HE COULD SAILING THROUGH THE AIR. LANDING ON ALL FOURS; BIG CAT BOUND AWAY INTO THE FOREST AS FAST AS HE COULD RUN. THE MEN GRABBED THEIR DOGS AND HELD THEM BACK AS HE RAN AWAY.

STEVE THOMPSON; KNEW FROM EXPERIENCE THAT THE CAT NEEDED REST. STEVE HAD SEEN COUGARS PUSHED TO THE LIMIT AT OTHER TIMES AND HE KNEW THAT THE RESULTS WOULDN'T TURN OUT GOOD IF THE CHASE CONTINUED. STEVE

HAD HUNTED MANY COUGARS IN MONTANA AND KNEW WELL THE ROUTINE OF WHAT TO DO AND WHAT *NOT* TO DO WHILE HUNTING MOUNTAIN LIONS.

HE KNEW HIS DOGS WOULD BE MORE THAN HAPPY TO CONTINUE TO CHASE THE CAT BUT THE DOGS HAD RAN MANY MILES AND THEY TOO WERE EXHAUSTED AND NEEDED REST. ALSO; HE KNEW THAT ANY FURTHER PURSUIT WOULD NOT ONLY JEOPARDIZE HIS DOGS BUT THE CAT MIGHT TURN AND ATTACK HIS HOUNDS SINCE BIG CAT HAD ALREADY WOUNDED A DOG.

BIG CAT RAN AS FAR AS HE COULD AWAY FROM THE MEN AND DOGS AND DIDN'T STOP UNTIL HE COULDN'T HEAR THEM ANYMORE. AFTER LISTENING INTENTLY FOR SOME TIME, HE CHECKED THE AREA LOOKING FOR A SAFE PLACE TO HIDE. THE WOODS WERE MAINLY FULL OF ASPEN AND AN OCCASIONAL BIRCH WITH LOW, ROLLING HILLS AND WET SWAMPY AREAS.

THIS TERRAIN MADE HIM REALLY MISS HIS HOMELAND WITH ITS HIGH BLUFFS AND CAVES WHERE HE COULD HIDE IN AS HE DID IN SOUTH DAKOTA. FOLLOWING A DEER TRAIL, HE SMELT FRESH DEER DROPPINGS AND IT REMINDED HIM OF THE DEER CARCASS HE HAD LEFT BEHIND AS HE BEGAN TO HUNT FOR FOOD.

THE SMELL OF WILD TURKEY CAUGHT HIS ATTENTION AND HE STARTED STALKING QUIETLY IN THAT DIRECTION HOPING FOR A MEAL. AS THE SCENT GOT STRONGER HE HEARD THE SOFT, GOBBLING SOUND AS THE TURKEYS SETTLED IN FOR THE NIGHT ON TREE BRANCHES. SEEING THAT THEY WERE SITTING IN THE TREE TOPS HE KNEW THAT HIS CHANCES WERE NEXT TO NIL THAT HE WOULD BE ABLE TO CATCH ONE OF THEM.

SUDDENLY, A MOVEMENT NEAR THE BASE OF THE TREE CAUGHT HIS EYE. QUICKLY, HE CROUCHED LOW AND WAITED TO SEE WHAT IT WAS. AS THE ANIMAL FLAPPED IT'S WINGS, BIG CAT COULD SEE THAT IT WAS A WILD TURKEY WITH SOMETHING WRONG WITH IT'S WING AND WASN'T ABLE TO FLY AWAY. IT WAS AN EASY CATCH FOR BIG CAT, SO WITH A FEW QUICK BOUNDS HE HAD A TURKEY MEAL TO ENJOY BECAUSE IT COULDN'T GET AWAY FROM HIM. AS HE SETTLED DOWN TO EAT; THE SQUAWKINGS OF THE TURKEYS IN THE TREES ABOVE DIDN'T STOP HIM FROM ENJOYING HIS MEAL.

GLANCING AROUND OFTEN TO SEE IF ALL WAS SAFE; BIG CAT FINISHED THE LAST MORSEL OF TURKEY AND SITTING ON HIS HUNCHES HE BEGAN TO CLEAN HIMSELF. FEATHERS WERE SCATTERED ALL AROUND HIM AS HE LICKED HIS LIPS AND CLEANED HIS FACE BY LICKING HIS FRONT PAWS THEN RUBBING HIS CHEEKS

WITH HIS PAW. THIS WAS ONE OF BIG CAT'S FAVORITE TIME TO RELAXED AS HE CLEANED HIMSELF UP AFTER A GOOD MEAL. HOWEVER, THE TURKEY'S CONTINUED SQUAWKING AND HE NEEDED TO FIND A BETTER PLACE TO REST.

GETTING UP, HE STRETCHED AND WALKED AWAY FROM THE TURKEYS. HE STARTED SEARCHING THE AREA FOR A SAFE PLACE TO HIDE FOR THE REST OF THE DAY. FINDING A SUITABLE TREE TO REST IN; BIG CAT JUMPED TEN FEET OFF THE GROUND, GRIPPING THE TREE WITH HIS SHARP CLAWS AND CLIMBED TO A BRANCH THAT WAS STRONG ENOUGH TO ALLOW HIM TO STRETCH OUT AND GET SOME NEEDED SLEEP.

HE HAD JUST DRIFTED OFF TO SLEEP WHEN A NOISE CLOSE TO HIM WOKE HIM UP—ABRUPTLY! IT WAS JUST A SQUIRREL; SCAMPERING OFF AFTER ALMOST STUMBLING ONTO BIG CAT BY ACCIDENT. IT HAD CLIMBED THE TREE FROM THE OTHER SIDE AND DIDN'T SEE BIG CAT UNTIL IT WAS ALMOST ON TOP OF HIM, THEN SCURRIED AWAY.

IT WAS LATE AFTERNOON; WHEN BIG CAT WOKE AND CLIMBED DOWN FROM THE TREE AND STARTED TO FOLLOWED A DEER TRAIL. FURTHER DOWN THE PATH THE WOODED AREA ALONG THE TRAIL NARROWED AS A FIELD CAME UP TO THE PINE TREES THAT GREW NEAR THE TRAIL AND A STEEP BANK WENT DOWN TO A CREEK ON THE OTHER SIDE.

BIG CATS HUNTING EXPERIENCE TOLD HIM THAT IF ANY DEER WERE TO TRAVEL THROUGH THE AREA THEY WOULD BE LIKELY TO COME DOWN THE TRAIL AND IF HE HID IN A TREE NEAR THE TRAIL HE COULD AMBUSH THEM THERE. SMELLING THE FRESH WATER IN THE BUBBLING BROOK NEXT TO HIM MADE HIM THIRSTY, SO HE WORKED HIS WAY DOWN THE STEP BANK AND LAPPED AT THE WATER. THE WATER WAS VERY REFRESHING TO HIS PALETTE AND IT SEEMED TO HELP REDUCE HIS HUNGER FOR THE MOMENT.

THEN AFTER LOOKING AROUND FOR ANY DANGER HE WORKED HIS WAY UP OUT OF THE CREEK BED AND FOUND A TREE WITH A VIEW WHERE HE COULD SEE ANY APPROACHING DEER. SCANNING THE AREA AGAIN FOR ANY MOTION OR SOUND; HE SPRANG UP THE TREE AND SETTLED INTO A COMFORTABLE POSITION ON A LIMB AND WAITED.

CHAPTER 3

DREAMING OF HOME

AFTER ABOUT AN HOUR WITHOUT ANY SIGNS OF DEER; BIG CAT DRIFTED OFF TO SLEEP WITH IMAGES OF THE EARLY YEARS OF LIFE COMING BACK TO HIM. HE AND HIS TWO SIBLINGS USED TO SCUFFLE OVER THE FRESH KILLS THAT THEIR MOTHER BOUGHT HOME AND HE REALLY ENJOYED THE SECURE FEELING HE HAD WHEN THEY ALL CUDDLED TOGETHER BY MOTHER NURSING AS SHE LICKED EACH ONE OF THEM. ALL THEY HAD TO CONCERN THEMSELVES WITH WAS PLAYING AND WAITING FOR MOTHER TO BRING THEM MORE FOOD.

HOWEVER, THEIR PEACEFUL FAMILY EXPERIENCE DIDN'T LAST LONG. ONE DAY A MALE MOUNTAIN LION FOUND THEIR DEN. IT IS CUSTOMARY FOR MALE "CATS" TO KILL KITTENS FROM ANOTHER MALES LITTER FOR TWO REASONS; ONE, TO GET RID OF ANY COMPETITION AND TWO, TO HAVE THEIR OWN LITTER WHEN THE FEMALE IS READY AGAIN. BIG CAT'S MOTHER FOUGHT FURIOUSLY, TO DEFEND THEM FROM HIM BUT AFTER THE FIGHT BETWEEN THE MALE COUGAR AND HIS MOTHER; ONLY HE AND HIS LITTLE SISTER WERE OK. ALTHOUGH REALLY FRIGHTENED, THE TWO OF THEM ESCAPED WITH THEIR LIVES FROM THE TERRIBLE ORDEAL. HOWEVER; THEIR BROTHER HAD BEEN KILLED AND THEIR MOTHER LAY BLEEDING, SEVERELY WOUNDED.

HE AND HIS SISTER STAYED CLOSE TO THEIR MOTHER ALL THE REST OF THE DAY AND THROUGH THE NIGHT AS SHE LAY WOUNDED ON THE GROUND. WHEN THE SUN CAME UP THE NEXT DAY AND HIS MOTHER HADN'T MOVED; THEY SENSED THAT SOMETHING WAS SERIOUSLY WRONG. INSTINCTIVELY, THEY SENSED

THAT THERE MOTHER WAS DEAD AND THEY WERE ALL ALONE TO FEND FOR THEMSELVES AND THEY NEEDED FOOD! FORTUNATELY; THEIR MOTHER HAD JUST BEGUN TEACHING THEM TO HUNT AS THEY HAD VENTURED AFTER HER AS SHE CAUGHT PREY FOR THEM.

SO AFTER SOME HESITATION; THE "YOUNG" BIG CAT RELUCTANTLY VENTURED OFF SEARCHING FOR FOOD. AFTER RUNNING BACK TO HER DEAD MOTHER TO SNIFF AND NUDGE AT HER, AGAIN AS SHE HAD DONE PREVIOUSLY; HIS LITTLE SISTER FOLLOWED HER BROTHER WHIMPERING AS SHE DID. AT FIRST; THEY WANDERED AIMLESSLY, LOOKING FOR WHATEVER THEY COULD FIND TO EAT. STUMBLED UPON THE REMAINS OF A RABBIT THAT FIRST DAY MY HAVE SAVED THEIR LIVES AS THEY WERE LUCKY TO FIND ANYTHING TO EAT!

IN THE BEGINNING, THEIR ATTEMPTS AT CATCHING GAME FAILED MORE TIMES THEN SUCCEEDED BUT WITH PRACTICE THEY GOT BETTER. AS THE TWO CATS GREW; CATCHING GAME BECAME A LITTLE EASIER AS THEY LEARNED TO CATCH MICE, THEN WITH PRACTICE, GROUND SQUIRRELS AND OTHER SMALL RODENTS.

THE LAND WHERE BIG CAT AND HIS SIBLINGS WERE BORN WAS MUCH DIFFERENT THEN NORTHERN WISCONSIN. THE TREES WERE FEW AND FAR BETWEEN IN THE HIGHER COUNTRY AND ONLY GREW BY THE FARM HOUSES IN THE LOW LAND WITH MILES OF OPEN, FLAT COUNTRY WHERE FARMERS PLANTED CORN, WHEAT, OATS, SOYBEANS AND OTHER CROPS.

ON THE WEST SIDE OF THE STATE OF SOUTH DAKOTA ARE THE BLACK HILLS WHERE BIG CAT AND HIS SIBLINGS WERE BORN IN A CAVE IN THE HIGH COUNTRY WITH CLIFFS AND STEEP LEDGES. WATER WASN'T ABUNDANT AND ONLY AN OCCASIONAL CREEK FLOWED OUT OF THE HILLS WHERE BIG CAT AND HIS SISTER GREW UP TOGETHER WITH ANTELOPE AND DEER ON THE PLAINS AND BIGHORNS SHEEP IN HIGH COUNTRY.

RUNNING AND SPLASHING THIS WAY AND THAT; BIG CAT AND HIS SISTER WERE TRYING TO CATCH SALMON IN THE CREEK ONE DAY BUT WEREN'T HAVING MUCH LUCK CATCHING ANY. HOWEVER; THEY WERE ENJOYING THE GAME AS THE FISH WIGGLED IN THE SHALLOW WATER IN FRONT OF THEM. AFTER SOME TIME; BIG CAT WAS ABLE TO GET HIS CLAWS INTO A FISH AND PULL IT ASHORE. HIS SISTER RAN OVER TO INVESTIGATE AND BIG CAT LET HER HAVE THE FISH. THEN HE WENT BACK AND WAS ABLE TO CATCH ANOTHER FISH IN HALF THE TIME.

THEY WERE BOTH GETTING THEIR BELLIES FULL WHEN A BIG GRIZZLY BEAR WALKED AROUND THE BEND IN THE CREEK TWENTY FEET AWAY FROM THEM! THEY ALL STARED AT ONE ANOTHER FOR A MOMENT IN SURPRISE; THEN THE BEAR STOOD UP ON ITS HIND LEGS AND THE YOUNG CATS TURNED AND RAN. BEING DRAWN BY THE SMELL OF FRESH FISH; THE GRIZZLY WAS AS SURPRISED TO MEET THE YOUNG COUGARS AS THEY WERE TO SEE HIM.

WHEN THE CUBS RAN AWAY THE GRIZZLY QUICKLY DROPPED TO ALL FOURS AND WALKED OVER TO THE FISH THEY LEFT BEHIND AND BEGAN TO EAT. BIG CAT KNEW THAT A GRIZZLY BEAR WAS DANGER AND BOUNDED OFF WITH HIS SISTER ONLY STOPPING A SAFE DISTANT AWAY TO WATCH THE GRIZZLY FINISH THEIR FISH.

ANOTHER DAY WHILE SCOUTING FOR FOOD, BIG CAT SAW A JACK RABBIT AND RACED AFTER IT. HIS SISTER TAGGING ALONG BEHIND HIM. HE WAS GAINING ON THE RABBIT WHEN IT MADE A QUICK TURN AND HE LOST GROUND AS IT RAN AWAY IN ANOTHER DIRECTION. DOUBLING BACK; HE RACED AFTER THE RABBIT CLOSING THE DISTANCE BETWEEN HIMSELF AND THE RABBIT AND JUST WHEN HE WAS ABOUT TO CATCH THE RABBIT, IT DOVE INTO A HOLE. SLIDING TO A STOP; THE YOUNG BIG CAT STOPPED AND SNIFFED AT THE HOLE.

ALL OF A SUDDEN; BIG CATS FACE WAS SHOVED INTO THE RABBIT'S DEN IN THE GROUND AS SOMETHING SLAMMED INTO HIM FROM BEHIND! HIS SISTER HAD BEEN TRYING SO HAD TO KEEP UP SHE DIDN'T SEE HER BROTHER STOP AND RAN INTO HIM! OFTEN TIMES AFTER EATING; THE TWO YOUNG COUGARS WOULD CHASES ONE ANOTHER AROUND AND PLAYFULLY PRACTICE THEIR HUNTING SKILLS ON ONE ANOTHER. THIS WOULD USUALLY END WITH THE TWO LYING SIDE BY SIDE GROOMING ONE ANOTHER AND FALLING ASLEEP.

AS THE MONTHS PASSED AND THE YOUNG COUGARS GREW, THEIR HUNTINGS SKILLS GOT TO THE POINT OF CATCHING AN OCCASIONAL MULE DEER. ONE DAY; BIG CAT LEFT HIS SISTER RESTING AND WENT HUNTING BY HIMSELF. HE FOUND A BLUFF THAT OVER-LOOKED A DEER TRAIL AND AFTER WAITING ON THE LEDGE FOR SOMETIME; A MULE DEER DOE AND FAWN CAME DOWN THE TRAIL TOWARDS THE LEDGE.

BIG CAT FLATTENED HIMSELF OUT ON THE ROCK AND PREPARED TO LEAP. JUST AS THE DEER WERE APPROACHING AND BIG CAT PREPARED TO LEAP; HIS SISTER CAME AROUND THE CORNER AND SCARED THE DEER AWAY. SHE HAD

AWOKEN FROM HER SLEEP AND CAME LOOKING FOR HER BROTHER STUMBLING UNTO HIS HUNT AND SPOILED THE CHANCE FOR A MEAL THAT DAY.

AFTER SPENDING ABOUT A YEAR TOGETHER; BIG CAT STARTED TO SENSE A CHANGE IN HIS SISTERS' INTERACTION WITH HIM. BECOMING MORE INDEPENDENT AND ALOOF, SHE WOULD WANDER OFF FOR A DAY OR TWO WITHOUT HIS KNOWING WHERE SHE WAS. ONE DAY HE SAW HER WITH ANOTHER COUGAR AND HER BEHAVIOR WAS ODD. AT FIRST; HE WAS ALARMED BUT THEN REALIZED THAT HIS SISTER WASN'T IN ANY TROUBLE. SHE SEEMED TO ENJOY THE OTHER CATS COMPANY AND IGNORED BIG CAT AS SHE PLAYED AND FROLICKED WITH THE OTHER COUGAR.

WHENEVER; BIG CAT ENCOUNTERED HIS SISTER AND THE OTHER MALE COUGAR TOGETHER; THE OTHER MALE SEEMED IRRITATED AND THREATENED TO HAVE BIG CAT AROUND. SO; AFTER WATCHING THE TWO OF THEM AT A DISTANT FOR SOMETIME; BIG CAT BEGAN TO SENSE THAT HIS SISTER HAD FOUND A MATE AND SHE COULD TAKE CARE OF HER SELF AND DIDN'T NEED HIS HELP ANYMORE.

CHAPTER 4

ON HIS OWN

IT WAS AT THIS TIME THAT BIG CAT REALIZED THAT HE WAS ON HIS OWN AND HAD TO FEND FOR HIMSELF. HE BEGAN TO HUNT WIDER AREAS AND DISCOVERED DIFFERENT PREY AS HE EXPLORED THE COUNTRY-SIDE. AS TIME WENT ON; HE FELT A NEED FOR COMPANIONSHIP AND STARTED LOOKING FOR A MATE.

IN HIS SEARCH; HE HAD TRAVELED FAR ENOUGH FROM HIS HOMELAND THAT THE TERRAIN WAS TOTALLY DIFFERENT FROM WHERE HE WAS RAISED. THE LAND WAS ALMOST COMPLETELY LEVEL WITH NO HIGH CLIFFS TO HIDE IN. SOMETHING DREW HIM IN THE DIRECTION AWAY FROM THE SETTING SUN AS HE CONTINUED SEARCHING AND EXPLORING.

INSTEAD OF HILLS WITH CLIFFS; ALL BIG CAT'S EYES COULD SEE NOW WERE FIELDS, FAR AND WIDE WITH ONLY A FEW TREES TO BE SEEN. WHEN HE DID TRY TO TAKE COVERAGE IN TREES; HE QUICKLY NOTICED THAT MOST GROUPS OF TREES HAD HOUSES IN OR NEAR THEM WHERE MAN LIVED.

AS BIG CAT CROSSED THROUGH THE FARM LAND; HE FOUND IT DIFFICULT TO STAY OUT OF SIGHT OF HUMANS. MORE THEN ONCE; HE HAD TO DASH INTO A DITCH OR HIDE IN A BRUSH PILE IN A FIELD TO ESCAPE HUMANS AND IT WAS IN THIS PART OF THE COUNTRY THAT HE HAD HIS FIRST ENCOUNTER WITH DOGS. HE HAD SEEN THEM FROM A DISTANCE BACK IN THE BLACK HILLS BUT HADN'T BEEN UP CLOSE TO THEM UNTIL HE HAPPENED UPON A DOG UNEXPECTEDLY ONE EVENING.

BOTH BIG CAT AND THE DOG WERE SHOCKED AND STOOD FROZEN IN THEIR TRACKS AS THEY STARED AT ONE ANOTHER. BUT WHEN THE DOG GOT AGGRESSIVE AND STARTED BARKING AT HIM; BIG CAT SNARLED BACK AND STRUCK OUT AT THE DOG WHEN IT CHARGED AT HIM. THE DOG SOON REALIZED THAT IT WAS NO MATCH FOR A COUGAR AS IT BACKED OFF AND RAN AWAY. THIS WAS VERY FORTUNATE FOR BIG CAT BECAUSE IF THE HOUND HAD CONTINUED BARKING AND DRAWN MAN TO THEM; HE WOULD HAVE BEEN HARD PRESSED TO FIND A TREE TO CLIMB!

REALIZING THAT THIS LAND WAS NOT FIT FOR HIM TO STAY OR LIVE IN; HE HID AND SLEPT DURING THE LIGHT OF DAY AND TRAVELED AS MUCH AS HE COULD DURING THE NIGHT CATCHING RABBITS AND SMALL PREY. WITHOUT THE HELP OF TREE LIMBS AND LEDGES; BIG CAT FOUND IT HARD TO AMBUSH DEER AND WAS GRATEFUL FOR THE OCCASIONAL ROAD KILLED.

BIG CAT HAD BEEN TRAVELING FOR ABOUT A YEAR AND HAD CROSSED THE DAKOTAS AND WAS ENTERING INTO CENTRAL MINNESOTA BY THIS TIME. ONE NIGHT AS HE TRAVELED LOOKING FOR FOOD; HE CAUGHT THE SCENT OF SOMETHING DEAD. CAREFULLY APPROACHING THE DEAD ANIMAL HE COULD SMELL THAT IT WASN'T A DEER BUT ANOTHER FAMILIAR SCENT.

WITH CLOSER INSPECTION; HE SAW THAT A DOG LAY DEAD IN A DITCH BY THE ROAD, POSSIBLY HIT BY A CAR. AS HE GOT CLOSER TO THE DEAD DOG; HE FELT A RISING SENSE OF RESENTMENT AND DISGUST THAT CAME FROM DEEP WITHIN HIM BECAUSE OF THE AGE OLD BATTLE BETWEEN CATS AND DOGS. AFTER SMELLING THE DOG; BIG CAT SIMPLY TURNED AND SPRAYED HIS SCENT ON THE DEAD DOG AND WALKED AWAY.

A FEW NIGHTS LATER AS HE TROTTED ACROSS A FARM FIELD; HE HEARD A PACK OF COYOTES AT A DISTANCE IN FRONT OF HIM HOWLING AT THE MOON. APPROACHING THE HOWLING COYOTES; HE WAS ABLE TO GET WITHIN ABOUT SEVENTY FIVE YARDS OF THEM WITHOUT THEM SEEING HIM. BREAKING INTO A RUN; HE RACED TOWARDS THEM AND THE COYOTES WERE TAKEN; TOTALLY BY SURPRISE AS BIG CAT BURST INTO THEIR MIDST.

THE SIGHT OF THE SCATTERING COYOTES WAS COMICAL TO WATCH AS THEY LITERALLY, TRIPPED OVER EACH OTHER IN THERE ATTEMPT TO GET AWAY FROM THE CHARGING COUGAR! BIG CAT HAD TO CHASE COYOTES AWAY FROM HIS KILLS MANY TIMES AND HE HELD NO LOVE FOR THE CREATURES. AFTER THE COYOTES

DISAPPEARED HE CONTINUED ON HIS WAY UNDISTURBED AND HE DIDN'T HEAR ANYMORE YAPPING FROM THEM THAT NIGHT.

NIGHT AFTER NIGHT, HE CONTINUED HIS JOURNEY UNTIL MORE TREES WERE BEGINNING TO SHOW ON THE HORIZON AS HE TRAVELED AWAY FROM THE SETTING SUN. WITH THE HELP OF MORE COVER; BIG CAT WAS LUCKY ENOUGH TO SURPRISE A YEARLING DEER AND OVER-TAKE IT. THE YEARLING HAD TRIED TO CROSS A BOGGY SWAMP AND BIG CAT'S BIG PAWS MADE IT EASIER FOR HIM TO CROSS THE BOG AND HE OVERTOOK THE DEER EASILY. BECAUSE IT WAS OUT OF THE SIGHT OF MAN HE SETTLED DOWN AND FILLED HIS BELLY STAYING BY HIS KILL RESTING AND EATING.

AS OFTEN HAPPENS IN THE WILD, CARNIVORES ARE DRAWN BY THE SCENT AND CAN'T RESIST A FREE MEAL. IN THE MID-MORNING; BIG CAT HEARD A NOISE THEN SAW A FOX AT ABOUT A HUNDRED YARDS AWAY AS IT FOLLOWED THE SCENT AND APPROACHED HIS KILL. LYING IN A CLUMP OF BRUSH ABOUT FIFTY FEET FROM HIS CATCH; HE SLOWLY GOT INTO THE CROUCHED POSITION AND WAITED FOR THE FOX TO GET NEAR.

AS THE FOX CAUTIOUSLY APPROACHED THE DEAD DEER; BIG CAT WAITED IN AMBUSH. WHEN THE FOX GOT TOO CLOSE TO THE KILL FOR BIG CATS LIKING; HE LAUNCHED HIMSELF OUT OF THE BRUSH IN PURSUIT OF IT. THE FOXES' REACTIONS WAS INSTANTANEOUS!

SPINNING AROUND IN HIS TRACKS; THE FOX RACED AS OFF AS FAST AS HE COULD WITH HIS TAIL UP AND A LITTLE SIDEWAYS, JUMPING BACK AND FORTH WITH THE AGILITY OF A GAZELLE. HAVING THE ADVANTAGE OF STARTING FIRST; BIG CAT QUICKLY GAINED ON THE FOX.

HOWEVER; BEING A LARGER ANIMAL, BIG CAT COULDN'T ZIGZAG BACK AND FORTH LIKE THE FOX AND SOON LOST GROUND IN THE CHASE. KNOWING THAT HIS MEAL WAS EXPOSED TO OTHER SCAVENGERS; HE LET THE FOX RACE OFF AND RETURNED TO HIS KILL.

THAT AFTERNOON ANOTHER VARMINT TIED TO STEAL HIS MEAL. THIS TIME CAUTION TOLD HIM TO HOLD BACK. IT WAS A SKUNK! LYING IN HIS HIDDEN SPOT; BIG CAT WAITED UNTIL IT APPROACHED NEAR ENOUGH, THEN STANDING UP TO SHOW HIMSELF, HE GROWLED AT THE SKUNK.

AT FIRST; HAVING VERY POOR EYE SIGHT, THE SKUNK DIDN'T KNOW *WHAT OR WHO* WAS GROWLING AT HIM. SO; GROWLING LOUDLY, BIG CAT STEPPED

FORWARD IN A FINAL ATTEMPT TO SCARE THE SKUNK OFF. MR. SKUNK DID WHAT COMES NATURALLY WHEN HE IS IN DANGER. SPINNING AROUND, HE HIKED HIS TAIL HIGH IN THE AIR AND SQUIRTED AT BIG CAT!

FORTUNATELY FOR BIG CAT; HE WAS OUT OF RANGE BUT THE STINK WAS OVER-POWERING. BIG CAT BACKED OFF PROTESTING LOUDLY WITH SNARLS AND GROWLS AND THE SKUNK BEING UNNERVED BY THE GROWLING, TURNED AND WADDLED AWAY.

WHEN THE SKUNK WAS GONE; BIG CAT, CAUTIOUSLY, APPROACHED THE CARCASS AND CLUTCHING A LEG BACKED UP DRAGGING THE KILL AWAY FROM THE RETCHED STINK. AFTER PULLING IT OVER FALLEN TREES AND OTHER OBSTACLES OUT OF THE RANGE OF THE STINK; HE STEPPED OVER THE DEER AND GOT A GOOD HOLD OF IT. WITH THE ANIMAL BETWEEN HIS LEGS, HE DRUG IT TO A BIG PINE TREE.

HIS MUSCLES BULGED AS HE STRAINED CLIMBING THE TREE WITH THE DEER IN HIS MOUTH AND HIS CLAWS RIPPED BARK OFF THE TREE AS HE REACHED FOR ANOTHER HOLD. FINALLY, REACHING A BIG LIMB HE PULLED THE KILL OVER THE LIMB AND RESTED. AS HE PANTED AND REGAINED HIS STRENGTH; HE SCANNED THE AREA FOR ANY DANGER.

THEN, AFTER POSITIONING THE DEER IN THE TREE SO THAT IT WOULDN'T FALL AND SATISFYING HIMSELF THAT ALL WAS OK; HE SETTLED DOWN TO EAT. HE STAYED IN THE TREE EATING ALL THAT HE WANTED FROM THE KILL UNTIL THERE WAS LITTLE LEFT. FINALLY; THIRST MADE HIM ABANDONED THE CARCASS AND CLIMBING DOWN THE TREE, HE HEADED FOR THE LITTLE POND THAT HE HAD SEEN FROM THE TREE AND DRANK.

CHAPTER 5

THE THIRD CHASE

THE SOUND OF BREAKING TWIGS, QUICKLY WOKE BIG CAT FROM HIS SLEEP AND BROUGHT HIM BACK TO REALITY OF WHERE HE WAS IN HIS RESTING SPOT IN THE TREE. HE REALIZED HE HAD BEEN DREAMING OF THE PAST AND HIS HUNGRY BROUGHT HIM TO THE PRESENT AS SOME DEER APPROACHED HIM DOWN THE TRAIL. IT HAD BEEN A FEW DAYS WITHOUT FOOD IN HIS STOMACH AND THE EARLY MORNING LIGHT SHOWED THAT THREE DEER WERE TRAVELING DOWN THE TRAIL IN HIS DIRECTION.

CROUCHING LOW IN THE TREE; HE WAITED IN ANTICIPATION FOR THE DEER TO DRAW CLOSER AS SALIVA DRIPPED FROM HIS MOUTH IN ANTICIPATION. AS THE DEER WERE COMING STRAIGHT AT HIM HE KNEW THAT HIS POSITION IN THE TREE WAS CLEARLY VISIBLE TO THEM IF THEY HAPPENED TO LOOKED UP AT HIM. HE; ALSO KNEW THAT THE DEER WOULD SEE HIM AND SPOOK IF HE TRIED TO MOVE INTO A BETTER POSITION, SO BIG CAT WAITED AND HOPED FOR THE BEST.

THEN THE DEER STOPPED JUST SHORT OF HIS LEAPING DISTANCE. POSSIBLY; THEY SAW HIM OR HEARD SOMETHING, OR WAS IT JUST THEIR NATURAL INSTINCT THAT MADE THEM EXTRA CAUTIOUS? BUT AFTER A FEW MINUTES THEY CONTINUED CAUTIOUSLY, WALKING TOWARDS HIM. BIG CAT LET THE FIRST PASS AND THE SECOND BUT WHEN THE LAST ONE WAS UNDER HIM; HE LEAPT.

INSTANTLY, ALL THE DEER BOUNDED AWAY AS THEY SAW HIM FLYING TOWARDS THEM. TWISTING IN THE AIR TO GET A BETTER ANGLE ON THE DEER

HE WAS ONLY ABLE TO GRAZE THE DEER WITH HIS LEFT PAW AS HAIR FLEW AND ALL THE DEER QUICKLY DISAPPEARED. ANOTHER MISS!

BIG CAT BARELY HAD TIME TO CHECK THE SURROUNDINGS WHEN HE HEARD THE DISTANT HOWLING OF HOUNDS—AGAIN! NOT SURE IF THEY WERE AFTER HIM; HE LISTENED INTENTLY TO THE SOUND OF THE BAYING HOUNDS. THE HOWLING ECHOED BACK AND FORTH THROUGH THE FOREST THEN FADED FOR A MOMENT; ONLY TO COME BACK STRONGER AND IN HIS DIRECTION.

FEELINGS OF DREAD AND ANGER RACED THROUGH HIM AS HE KNEW WHAT LAY AHEAD. TURNING; HE BOUNDED DOWN THE DEER TRAIL AWAY FROM THE HOUNDS. AFTER RUNNING FOR SOME DISTANCE THE SCENT OF WATER MADE HIM THIRSTY AND HE STOPPED TO DRINK AT THE CREEK.

AFTER A QUICK DRINK; HE LISTENED FOR THE DOGS AND HOPED THAT THEY WEREN'T AFTER HIM AGAIN BUT THEIR HOWLING WAS GETTING LOUDER SO HE RAN ON. RUNNING ALONG THE EDGE OF THE CREEK, DODGING TREES AND HANGING LIMBS, HIS LEAN, MUSCLES BEGAN TO ACHE FOR OXYGEN. AS HIS BODY NEARED EXHAUSTION; HE SUDDENLY FELT NEW VIGOR AS ADRENALINE PUMPED THROUGH HIS VEINS STIRRING HIM ON.

THE HOUNDS ECHOING VOICES RESOUNDED THROUGH THE TREES AS BIG CAT RACED AHEAD OF THEM ALONG THE CREEK. SEEING THE SUN SPARKLING OFF THE CLEAR BROOK WATER; HE RECALLED THAT WATER HAD HELPED HIM EVADE DOGS BEFORE AS THEY PURSUED HIM, SO BIG CAT PADDED DOWN INTO THE STREAM AND BEGAN WADING IN THE WATER DOWN THE CREEK AWAY FROM THE HOUNDS.

OCCASIONALLY; LEAPING OVER FALLEN TREES AND BOUNDING OFF OF BOULDERS, HE CONTINUED AS FAR AS HE COULD UNTIL THE WATER DEEPENED TO HIS CHEST. AFTER TRAVELING AS FAR DOWN THE CREEK AS HE POSSIBLY COULD TO ESCAPE THE DOGS TRAILING HIM; HE LEAPT UP ON THE FAR BANK AWAY FROM THE HOUNDS AND CONTINUED RUNNING ON.

AFTER STANDING AND LISTENING FOR THE BAYING OF THE HOUNDS; HE LOPED TOWARDS THE TALLER TREES AHEAD OF HIM. TRAVELING ABOUT A MILE; HE CAME UPON A STEEP RAVINE THAT LEAD DOWN INTO A SWAMP. ON THE OTHER SIDE OF THE RAVINE HE COULD SEE A HOUSE AT A DISTANCE BUT OVER THE RAVINE WAS A LOW FIELD THAT LED TO MORE TREES.

AS HE STOPPED TO LISTEN FOR THE PURSUING HOUNDS; BIG CAT COULD TELL THAT THEIR BAYING WAS MORE DISTANT AND HE HOPED THEY HAD LOST HIS TRAIL. BUT PAST EXPERIENCE TOLD HIM THAT HE HAD TO CONTINUE RUNNING TO MAKE SURE TO DISTANCE HIM SELF AS MUCH AS POSSIBLE FROM THEM. MAKING HIS WAY DOWN THE RAVINE; HE CLIMBED THE OTHER SIDE AND HEADED ACROSS THE FIELD NEAR THE SWAMP.

AS HE LOOPED ALONG; SOMETHING CAUGHT HIS EYE TO HIS RIGHT AS HE HEARD A HUMAN VOICE AND SAW A MAN ON THE OTHER SIDE OF THE FIELD. QUICKENING HIS SPEED AND TAKING LONGER JUMPS; HE RACED AWAY ACROSS THE FIELD TO THE NEAREST SHELTER OF TREES. ONCE INTO THE WOODS; BIG CAT CONTINUED RUNNING WANTING TO GET AS FAR AWAY FROM THE TRAILING DOGS AS HE COULD.

TRAVELING AT THE SPEED HE WAS; HE BEGAN TO TIRE AND HAD TO EXERT EXTRA EFFORT TO DODGE TREES, BRUSH AND FALLEN OBSTACLES. THE CONTINUOUS RUNNING WAS CAUSING HIS LUNGS TO HURT BUT HE KNEW HE HAD TO MAKE AS MUCH DISTANCE BETWEEN HIMSELF AND THE PACK AS POSSIBLE. HE CONTINUED TO RUN ON MILE AFTER MILE TURNING AWAY FROM THE SCENT OF HUMANS IN HIS PATH, THEN BACK THE OTHER DIRECTION AS OTHER SCENTS OF HUMAN DANGER ENTERED HIS NOSE.

FEELING HIS LUNGS BURSTING, BIG CAT KNEW HE NEEDED TO REST. AFTER CROSSING THROUGH SOME THICK WOODS AND FEELING A LITTLE MORE SECURE HE SAW A LARGE TREE IN FRONT OF HIM AND HARDLY SLOWED HIS PACE AS LEAPED UP CLAWING THE TREE ON BOTH SIDE WITH HIS POWERFUL FRONT PAWS PUSHING HIMSELF UP WITH HIS BACK LEGS. PANTING, HE SETTLED DOWN ON A LIMB AND LISTENED FOR THE DOGS.

THE LEAD DOG WAS CONFUSED WHEN IT ARRIVED AT THE CREEK WHERE BIG CAT HAD ATTEMPTED TO LOSE THEM BECAUSE IT COULDN'T PICK UP THE TRAIL RIGHT AWAY. SO; IT BEGAN TO SNIFF AROUND THE AREA, RUNNING BACK AND FORTH SEARCHING FOR THE CAT'S TRAIL.

AS THE PACK ARRIVED BEHIND HIM; THEY ALL BEGAN TO CIRCLE AND SEARCH THE AREA UP AND DOWN THE CREEK, BARKING AS THEY LOOKED FOR BIG CAT'S SCENT. THE SEARCH GREW WIDER AND FURTHER DOWN THE CREEK AS THEY CONTINUED SNIFFING. THE LEAD DOG; BEING MORE DETERMINED, BEGAN TO

SEARCH IN A LARGER CIRCLE THAN THE OTHERS AND *BY ACCIDENT* CAME UPON THE SPOT WHERE BIG CAT HAD CLIMBED UP ON THE BANK OF THE CREEK.

WITH A LOUD, RESOUNDING HOWL; HE INFORMED THE OTHER HOUNDS THAT HE HAD FOUND BIG CATS TRAIL AND WAS SIGNALING THEM TO FOLLOW HIM!

BIG CAT HEARD THE HOUNDS BARKING GROW LOUDER AND LOUDER AS THEY SCRAMBLED THROUGH THE WOODS ON HIS SCENT TRAIL. HAVING GOT HIS BREATH BACK AND FEELING REVIVED; HE QUICKLY CLIMBED DOWN THE TREE AND RACED OFF AS HIS POWERFUL HINDLEGS PUSHED HIM FORWARD IN LONG STRIDES. HE RAN THROUGH WOODED AREAS WITH BIG OAK TREES, THEN AFTER THAT HE WENT THROUGH GROVES OF SMALL ASPEN TREES GROWING IN CLEARED FOREST AREAS AND PAST A HOUSE WHERE A FAMILY DOG SAW HIM AND BEGAN TO BARK.

BIG CAT CONTINUED TO RUN, GLANCING BACK OVER HIS SHOULDER TO SEE IF THE DOG WAS PURSUING HIM. THE DOG DID START TOWARDS HIM BUT WAS JERKED BACK BY THE CHAIN ATTACHED TO HIS COLLAR.

AS THE DOG CONTINUED TO BARK, BIG CAT KNEW THAT HE NEEDED TO DISTANT HIMSELF AS FAR FROM MAN AND HIS DOGS AS POSSIBLE. AS HE RACED AWAY FROM THE DOG HE CAME UPON A LARGE PLANTATION OF PINES WHICH TOWERED OVER HIM. NOT LIKING THE OPEN AREA UNDER THE BIG PINES BECAUSE OF THE CHANCE OF BEING SEEN, BIG CAT DIDN'T SLOW DOWN UNTIL HE WAS ONCE AGAIN INTO A THICK, BRUSHY AREA FULL OF TREES.

AFTER RUNNING FOR MILES, HIS MUSCLES BEGAN TO ACHE FROM EXHAUSTION AND AS HE JUMPED A LOG HE LANDED ON A SLIPPERY SPOT AND HIS FRONT PAWS SLID OUT FROM UNDER HIM BUT WITH HIS CAT-LIKE AGILITY BIG CAT RECOVERED HIS BALANCE AND CONTINUED ON. THIS EXHAUSTED HIM MORE AND HE KNEW HE HAD TO STOP RUNNING AND SAW A BIG OAK AHEAD WITH LARGE LIMBS AND WITH HIS LAST BIT OF STRENGTH HE CLAWED HIS WAY UP HIGH IN THE TREE.

CHAPTER 6

TREED AGAIN

THIS TIME HE HAD NO STRENGTH TO FLEE FROM THE HOUNDS AS THEY CLOSED IN ON HIM. HE JUST CROUCHED AS LOW AS HE COULD ON THE LIMB AND WATCHED THE DOGS COME BOUNDING DOWN ON HIM ALONG HIS TRAIL. SEEING HIM IN THE TREE THEY HOWLED IN EXCITEMENT AT THEIR CATCH. THE LEAD HOUND LOOKED UP AND TRIED TO CLIMB UP THE TREE BUT SLIPPED BACK AS HE BAYED EVEN LOUDER SEEING BIG CAT CLOSE ABOVE HIM.

THE OTHER HOUNDS FOLLOWED THE LEAD DOG AS THEY CONTINUED BARKING AND JUMPING UP AND DOWN AT THE BASE OF THE TREE. THE BARKING AND YAPPING WAS OVER-POWERING FOR BIG CAT AS HE SNARLED DOWN AT THE DOGS WITH HIS EARS FLATTEN IN ANGER. THE COMMOTION WAS SO DISTRACTING FOR BIG CAT THAT HE DIDN'T SEE THE MEN APPROACH BELOW

THEN IGNORING THE HOUNDS, BIG CAT TURNED AND SNARLED AT STEVE THOMPSON AND FRIENDS AS THEY APPROACHED THE TREE. THIS WAS THE THIRD TIME IN A FEW DAYS THAT HE HAD BEEN DRIVEN UP A TREE BY "MAN'S HOUNDS" AND HE WAS IRRITATED! AFTER STANDING BELOW HIM FOR AWHILE; ONE MAN POINTED A FIRE STICK AT HIM AGAIN AND BIG CAT SNARLED DOWN AT THE MAN KNOWING WHAT WAS ABOUT TO HAPPEN.

THE STICK EXPLODED AND BIG CAT FELT A STING IN HIS HIND QUARTERS. HE SPUN HIS HEAD AROUND GRABBING THE DART IN HIS MOUTH BITING IT AND TOSSING IT AWAY FROM HIM. AS THE MEN STOOD LOOKING UP AT HIM; HE TRIED TO CLIMB TO A SAFER SPOT AWAY FROM DANGER. THE ATTEMPT WAS FRUITLESS;

AS THE LIMB ONLY BENT UNDER HIM AS HE TRIED TO CLIMB HIGHER IN THE TREE, SO HE BACKED DOWN TO A SAFER POSITION.

AFTER A FEW MINUTES HE BEGAN TO FEEL STRANGE? HIS SIGHT STARTED TO GET UNCLEAR AND HIS BALANCE WAS NOT STEADY ANYMORE. HE SLUNK CLOSER TO THE LIMB SINKING HIS CLAWS INTO THE TREE AS FEAR AND ANGER ROSE IN HIM AND THE MEN WALKED AROUND THE TREE LOOKING UP AT HIM. HE COULD HEAR THERE TALKING BUT HE COULDN'T SEE THEM VERY WELL.

TO HIS SURPRISE, A MAN WALKED OVER TO THE TREE TRUNK AND BEGAN TO CLIMB UP TOWARDS HIM. THREATENED AND CONFUSED BY THIS; BIG CAT JUMPED TO A NEARBY LIMB TRYING TO CLIMB HIGHER AND SNARLING DOWN AT THE MAN. THE MAN STAYED WHERE HE WAS REALIZING THE DANGER OF APPROACHING ANY CLOSER TO BIG CAT. THE MAN AND THE CAT STARED AT ONE ANOTHER IN A STAND–OFF FOR A MOMENT AND THE OUTCOME WAS UNSURE BUT BIG CAT ONLY WANTED TO DISTANCE HIMSELF FROM THE SITUATION AND GET AWAY FROM THE SITUATION.

REALIZING THAT HE WAS TRAPPED IN THE TREE; BIG CAT KNEW HE HAD TO FLEE, SO TURNING AWAY FROM THE MAN HE LEAPT FOR THE GROUND. HIS LEGS DIDN'T RESPOND AS USUAL AND HE LANDED HARD! STRUGGLING TO RUN, HE FELT

LIKE HE WAS RUNNING IN A DREAM AND COULD HARDLY MOVE. HIS MUSCLES DIDN'T RESPOND TO HIS COMMAND TO RUN AND HE FELT NUMB AS HE FORCED HIMSELF TO RUN AWAY FROM THE MEN WHO WERE SHOUTING BEHIND HIM.

HIS LEGS DIDN'T WANT TO MOVE AS THEY SHOULD AND THIS NEW FEAR OF NOT BEING IN CONTROL OF HIS BODY MADE HIM PUSH HIMSELF EVEN HARDER TO GET AWAY. STUMBLING OVER FALLEN TREES; HE CONTINUED ON AND AFTER RUNNING FOR ABOUT A HALF–MILE AND NOT SEEING THE HOUNDS AFTER HIM, BIG CAT STOPPED TO REST. HIS BODY FELT HEAVY AND HIS MIND WASN'T CLEAR. HIS LEGS WERE GIVING OUT FROM UNDER HIM AS HE FORCED HIS BODY TOWARDS A CLUMP OF HEAVY BRUSH AND PUSHED HIS WAY IN. FALLING FORWARD; HE PASSED OUT!

CHAPTER 7

BETTER DAYS

WHEN BIG CAT BECAME CONSCIOUS HE WASN'T SURE WHERE HE WAS OR WHAT HAPPENED TO HIM? SLOWLY HIS MIND CLEARED AND HE REMEMBERED THE MEN AND THE HOUNDS CHASING AFTER HIM. THEN; STRUGGLING TO GET UP, HE SLOWLY STEPPED OUT OF THE BRUSH AND LOOKED AROUND. HE COULDN'T HEAR OR SMELL ANYTHING UNUSUAL SO HE WALKED OUT INTO A CLEARING WHERE HE COULD SEE BETTER. HIS BODY ACHED AND HIS HIND QUARTER WAS SORE WHERE THE NEEDLE HAD HIT HIM AND HE SAT AND LICKED IT.

AFTER CLEANING HIMSELF UP, BIG CAT FELT THE PAINS OF HUNGER AND STARTED CHECKING THE BREEZE FOR ANY SCENT OF FOOD. HIS NOSE PICKED UP A DISTANT ODOR OF MEAT AND HE STARTED WALKING IN THAT DIRECTION. THE SORE MUSCLES SLOWED HIM DOWN BUT HE HAD TO EAT AND CONTINUED THROUGH THE BIG ASPEN TREES AND AROUND THE THICK HAZEL BRUSH FOR SOMETIME BEFORE COMING OVER A RIDGE AND SEEING THE CARCASES OF DEAD ANIMALS ON THE BOTTOM OF A RAVINE BELOW HIM.

MAKING HIS WAY DOWN THE RAVINE; PAST THE BRIER PATCH AND AROUND THE OLD, RUSTY REFRIGERATOR AND OTHER DISCARDED JUNK, BIG CAT WALKED UP TO THE CARCASSES AND SNIFFED THEM. THERE SEEMED TO BE PLENTY OF BONES AND MEAT SCRAPS PILED UP AND AS HE SETTLED HIMSELF DOWN ON HIS BELLY HE BEGAN CHEWING ON THE MEAT. HE HAD BEEN EATING FOR SOME TIME WHEN HE HEARD A CAR ON THE ROAD ABOVE. LOOKING UP HE SAW THE CAR SLOW DOWN WITH IT'S LIGHTS SHINING ON HIM AND AS QUICKLY AS HE

COULD HE TURNED AND DASHED FOR COVER WITH HIS LONG TAIL STRETCHING OUT BEHIND HIM.

JIM SMITH, THE FARMER WHO OWNED THE LAND THAT BIG CAT WAS ON WAS A VERY SELF-RELIANT MAN RAISING AND SLAUGHTERING HIS OWN MEAT. JIM HAD JUST RECENTLY HARVESTED A STEER AND A PIG FOR WINTER MEAT AND DISCARDED THE REMAINS OVER THE RAVINE. JIM'S FRIEND, BILL HAD COME TO VISIT JIM AND IT WAS HE WHO HAD JUST DRIVEN DOWN THE ROAD. BILL HAPPENED TO GLANCE DOWN THE RAVINE AS HE PASSED AND DEFINITELY SAW A LARGE, LIGHT-BROWN CAT CROUCHED DOWN AND AS IT DASHED OFF HE SAW THE LONG TAIL.

BILL WAS SO SURPRISED BY SEEING THE COUGAR THAT HE DIDN'T EVEN TELL JIM ABOUT IT. HE FELT THAT HIS FRIEND WOULDN'T BELIEVE HIM AND DIDN'T TELL ANYONE ABOUT IT FOR SOME TIME. BIG CAT WAITED IN THE THICK BRUSH MAKING SURE THERE WASN'T ANY DANGER BEFORE COMING BACK OUT TO EAT. IT WAS GET DARKER AND HE FELT MORE AT EASE AS THE SHADOWS BEGAN TO APPEAR.

AFTER FEASTING ON THE CARCASSES HE STAYED NEAR THE MEAT FINDING A HIGH, STEEP BANK WITH A OVER-HANG TO HIDE IN AND SLEEP DURING THE DAY. HE RETURNED FOR THREE DAYS EATING THE CARCASSES UNTIL THE FLIES LAID MAGGOTS AND THE OVER-POWERING ODOR WAS TOO MUCH FOR HIS SENSITIVE NOSE.

CHAPTER 8

TOM'S HOUSE CATS

TOM RINGTON'S HOUSE CATS WOKE HIM UP WITH A SCREECH AS THEY FOUGHT OVER FOOD OUTSIDE. TOM HAD ADOPTED A STRAY CAT A FEW MONTHS BEFORE AND THE NEXT THING HE KNEW HE HAD 2 OR 3 STRAYS CATS HANGING AROUND OUTSIDE HIS HOUSE. THEN, BEFORE LONG THERE WAS A BUNCH OF THEM.

BEING A GENTLE-SPIRITED PERSON; TOM COULDN'T BRING HIMSELF TO ELIMINATE THEM SO HE WAS STUCK WITH THEM! HE DID ASK A FRIEND TO HELP HIM GET RID OF SOME OF THE CATS BUT THEY WERE SO QUICK TO HIDE THEY ONLY GOT RID OF A COUPLE.

WHILE TOM WAS OUT FEEDING THE CATS ONE MORNING; HE NOTICED STRANGE-LOOKING TRACKS ACROSS HIS SOUTH LAWN OUT BY THE ROAD THAT RUNS NEXT TO SAND LAKE. WHEN HE WALKED OUT TO TAKE A CLOSER LOOK; HE WAS SURPRISED TO SEE THAT THEY APPEARED TO BE A MOUNTAIN LION TRACKS!

TOM HAD SEEN WHAT HE THOUGHT TO BE A COUGAR A FEW YEARS BACK WHILE HUNTING DEER. HE HAD BEEN SITTING IN HIS DEER STAND FOR A COUPLE HOURS WHEN HE HEARD A NOISE OFF TO HIS LEFT. TURNING TO SEE WHAT IT WAS; HE WAS SHOCKED TO SEE A BIG CAT CLIMBING OVER A PILE OF WOOD SCRAPS AND THEN DISAPPEAR. HE HAD HEARD STORIES FROM OTHER HUNTERS ABOUT MOUNTAIN LIONS IN THE AREA BUT HADN'T ANY EVIDENCE UNTIL THEN.

SOMETIME LATER WHILE DRIVING HIS CAR, TOM HAD A PASSING GLANCE AT WHAT POSSIBLY COULD OF BEEN A COUGAR AND, THEN ANOTHER TIME YEARS

LATER WHILE HUNTING HE THOUGHT HE SAW A MOUNTAIN LION IN THE WOODS. HOWEVER; BOTH TIMES HE DIDN'T GET A GOOD VIEW OF THE ANIMAL.

REFLECTING BACK ON HIS DEER HUNTING EXPERIENCES, TOM REMEMBERED THE MORNING WHEN A COUPLE DOGS WERE CHASING AN ALBINO DOE BY SAND LAKE AND IN AN ATTEMPT TO ESCAPE THE DOGS, THE DOE SWAM ACROSS THE LAKE. IT WAS EARLY SPRING AND THE WATER WAS PRETTY COLD, YET THE DOE MADE IT ALL THE WAY ACROSS TO THE OTHER SIDE.

HOWEVER; THE DOE WAS GETTING UP IN YEARS AND THE FACT THAT SHE WAS PREGNANT EXHAUSTED HER ALL THE MORE AND SHE STUMBLED UP ON THE OTHER SIDE AND DIED! TOM HAD SEEN THE DOE AROUND FOR A NUMBER OF YEARS AND WAS SAD TO SEE HER PASS AWAY IN SUCH A PITIFUL WAY.

BIG CAT HAD WALKED ACROSS TOM'S YARD THAT NIGHT BUT AFTER SCENTING TOM'S DOG HE CONTINUED ON SEARCHING FOR FOOD ACROSS THE ROAD. WALKING OVER THE ROAD AND ONTO THE SANDY BEACH; BIG CAT SEARCHED FOR FISH, STRAY CRABS OR ANY EDIBLE THING. NOT FINDING ANYTHING; HE WANDERER OVER TO THE NEAREST HOUSE AND FOUND SOME SCRAPS IN THE YARD. ALL THE LIGHTS WERE OUT IN THE HOUSES SO BIG CAT FELT CONFIDENT THAT HE WAS SAFE EXPLORING NEAR THE HUMAN DOMAIN.

TRAVELING ON PAST THE NEXT HOUSE; HE SMELT AN ODD ODOR AND FOUND SOME DOG FOOD IN A BOWL OUTSIDE. SNIFFING IT; HE CAREFULLY TASTED THE FOOD AND FOUND IT WAS TASTY. AFTER LICKING THE BOWL CLEAN HE HEADED OFF INTO THE FOREST.

BIG CAT TRAVELED FOR MILES OVER ROLLING HILLS AND LOW, MARSHY AREAS DURING THE NIGHT AND FOUND VERY LITTLE TO EAT. WHEN THE SUN BEGAN TO RISE IN THE EAST HE STARTED LOOKING FOR SHELTER. IN THE LATE AFTERNOON; HE AWOKE IN THE TREE THAT HE HAD FOUND THAT MORNING TO REST IN AND THE STRONG ODOR OF PINE FILLED HIS NOSE AS HE SETTLED ON THE LIMB ABOUT TWENTY FEET OFF THE GROUND AND SCANNED THE AREA.

PICKING UP THE SCENT OF HUMANS FROM A DISTANCE ALERTED HIS ATTENTION BUT ANOTHER SCENT OF FOOD DREW HIM IN THAT DIRECTION. AS HE APPROACHED A LONE HOUSE IN A WOODED AREA; BIG CAT FELT CONFIDENT AS HE WALKED TO THE EDGE OF THE FOREST FOLLOWING THE ALLURING SCENT THAT HAD DRAWN HIM THERE.

CHAPTER 9

CHICKEN DINNER

THE SMELL OF CHICKENS HAD DRAWN HIM TO THE HUMANS' HOUSE AND HUNGER MADE HIM BOLD AS HE SAT DOWN ON HIS HUNCHES IN PLAIN SIGHT AND WATCHED A MAN CHOP WOOD. HE COULD SEE THE CHICKENS WALKING AROUND THE YARD AND ONLY HIS FEAR OF HUMANS STOPPED HIM FROM GOING AFTER THEM. A MAN CHOPPING WOOD STOPPED AND LOOKED AT HIM BUT DIDN'T MAKE ANY THREATENING MOVES; SO BIG CAT JUST SAT AND WATCHED HIM WORK. AS THE SUN STARTED TO GO DOWN THE MAN FINISHED HIS CHOPPING AND BIG CAT WATCHED THE MAN PUT THE CHICKENS IN THEIR HEN HOUSE FOR THE NIGHT AND GO INTO HIS HOUSE.

HE WAITED UNTIL IT WAS COMPLETELY DARK TO MAKE SURE ALL WAS CLEAR BEFORE WALKING OVER TO THE HEN HOUSE. SNIFFING AROUND THE CHICKEN PEN; HE LOOKED FOR THE EASIEST WAY TO GET INTO IT. THE CHICKENS HAD JUMPED UP ON THEIR ROUSTS AND WERE SETTLING IN FOR THE NIGHT.

FINDING A WEAK SPOT IN THE FENCE; BIG CAT TORE AT IT WITH HIS FRONT PAW. THE CHICKENS BEGAN TO CLUCK AS HE PULLED AND STRETCHED THE FENCE. THE FENCE DIDN'T GIVE WAY SO BIG CAT BEGAN TO WALK AROUND THE WHOLE ENCLOSURE LOOKING FOR A BETTER ENTRANCE INTO THE CHICKEN PEN.

THE ODOR OF CHICKENS WAS VERY STRONG AND HE BECAME MORE DETERMINED THEN EVER TO GET INTO THE PEN AS HE WALKED AROUND THE HEN HOUSE. FINDING A LOOSE BOARD; HE BEGAN PULLING IT WITH HIS PAW AND IT GAVE WAY FROM THE SHED WITH A CRACKING SOUND!

THE HOLE WASN'T BIG ENOUGH FOR HIM TO ENTER; SO BIG CAT STUCK HIS PAW INSIDE AND PULLED HARD ON THE OTHER BOARDS. THE BOARDS DIDN'T GIVE AWAY; SO HE REACHED AS FAR AS HE COULD INSIDE THE PEN AND SWUNG HIS PAW AROUND HOPING TO CATCH A CHICKEN.

BY THIS TIME THE CHICKENS WERE PRETTY EXCITED; SQUAWKING AND CLUCKING AND BIG CAT SENSED THAT HE HAD TO HURRY BECAUSE THE MAN MIGHT COME OUT OF THE HOUSE TO CHECK OUT WHY THE CHICKENS WERE SQUAWKING.

SO; STRETCHING HIS REACH FURTHER INTO THE PEN; HE CONTINUED SWINGING IT AROUND IN HOPES OF CATCHING SOMETHING. THE CHICKENS WERE ABOVE HIM ON THE ROUST BUT ONE HAD JUMPED DOWN TO THE FLOOR IN IT'S EXCITEMENT AND BEING DARK IT WALKED WITHIN REACH OF THE PAW. BIG CAT GRABBED IT WITH HIS CLAWS AND PULLING IT OUT OF THE PEN AND RAN OFF WITH THE CHICKEN IN HIS MOUTH.

AFTER FINISHING THE CHICKEN, BIG CAT FELT TEMPORALLY SATISFIED AND WENT BACK TO HIS TREE DEN THAT HE HAD SLEPT IN THE DAY BEFORE. HE WAS STILL FEELING THE AFTER-AFFECTS FROM THE HOUND CHASE AND SLEPT ALL THROUGH THE NIGHT AND RESTED THE NEXT DAY UNTIL DUSK WHEN HUNGRY AWOKE HIM. REMEMBERING THE CHICKEN PEN, HE RETURNED TO TRY TO GET ANOTHER CHICKEN.

WAITING UNTIL DARK; HE RETURNED TO THE SAME SPOT IN THE HEN HOUSE AND FOUND IT WAS COMPLETELY COVERED UP WITH BOARDS. WITH A LOW GROWL OF DISAPPROVAL; HE BEGAN TO LOOK FOR ANOTHER WAY INTO THE HEN HOUSE. AS HE CIRCLED THE CHICKEN PEN, HE COULD TELL THAT IT WOULDN'T BE AS EASY AS THE NIGHT BEFORE.

AFTER PULLING AT THE FENCE AND A FEW BOARDS WITHOUT SUCCESS; BIG CAT WAS LOSING PATIENCE AND PULLED EVEN HARDER ON A BOARD THAT HIS CLAWS HAD GOTTEN AROUND. THE BOARD STARTED TO GIVE WAY SO HE SUNK HIS TEETH INTO THE BOARD AND YANKED . . . THE BOARD BROKE LOOSE WITH A LOUD CRACK BUT HE STILL DIDN'T HAVE ENOUGH ROOM TO GET INSIDE, SO HE REACHED IN AGAIN.

THIS TIME HE DIDN'T FEEL A CHICKEN; SO REACHING AS FAR AS HE COULD INTO THE HEN HOUSE HE PUSHED HARDER THAN EVER STRUGGLING TO GRAB SOMETHING. ALL THE NOISE AND MOVEMENT HAD STARTLED THE CHICKENS AND

THE SQUAWKING INCREASED. THIS ONLY EXCITED BIG CAT MORE AS HE FOUGHT TO CLUTCH THEM IN HIS PAWS.

SUDDENLY; WITH A LOUD CRACKING SOUND THE BOARD GAVE WAY AND HE FOUND HIMSELF INSIDE THE CHICKEN HOUSE WHICH CAUSED THE CHICKENS TO PANIC AND FLY AGAINST THE WIRE-WINDOWS TRYING TO ESCAPE. FEATHERS FLEW IN ALL DIRECTIONS AS BIG CAT SCRAMBLED TO GRAB THE CHICKENS. THEY WERE TRAPPED AND HE DIDN'T HAVE ANY PROBLEM HOOKING ONE AFTER ANOTHER WITH HIS CLAWS AND FINISHING THEM OFF. BIG CAT COULDN'T CATCH AND TAKE THEM ALL WITH HIM BUT HE DID MANAGER TO TAKE TWO AT A TIME IN HIS MOUTH AS HE FLED THE SCENE OF PANICKING CHICKENS AND FLYING FEATHERS!

HAVING FOUND A WAY TO GET SUCH AN EASY MEAL; BIG CAT CAME BACK THE NEXT NIGHT AND DISCOVERED THE HEN HOUSE JUST AS HE HAD LEFT IT, BROKEN OPEN WITH DEAD CHICKENS ALL OVER. THE OWNERS OF THE CHICKENS HAD GIVEN UP AND LEFT EVERYTHING THE WAY BIG CAT HAD LEFT IT.

THE OWNERS HAD AN ALTERNATIVE REASON FOR NOT CLEANING UP THE MESS WHICH BIG CAT DISCOVERED LATER. THE SITUATION SUITED BIG CAT FINE AND AFTER CHECKING THE AREA TO SEE IF IT WAS SAFE, HE SETTLED DOWN TO EAT THE DEAD CHICKENS RIGHT WHERE THEY LAY. ONE AFTER ANOTHER, HE DEVOURED THEM UNTIL HE BEGAN TO FEEL FULL. THEN; GRABBING THE COUPLE THAT WERE LEFT IN HIS MOUTH HE WENT BACK TO HIS LAIR.

AFTER RESTING AND EATING THE CHICKENS HE HAD TAKEN WITH HIM; BIG CAT WAS DRAWN BACK TO THE CHICKEN PEN HOPING FOR ANOTHER EASY MEAL. HIS NOSE TOLD HIM THAT HE SHOULD BE MORE CAUTIOUS BECAUSE IT PICKED UP A NEW SCENT, SO APPROACHING WELL AFTER DARK HE DISCOVERED THE SCENT OF DOGS PRESENT ON THE SITE.

AS HE SURVEYED THE AREA HIS NOSE PICKED UP FAMILIAR SCENTS THAT FLOODED HIS BRAIN WITH MEMORIES OF HIS OLD ENEMIES—THE HOUNDS. IT APPEARED THE OWNERS HAD HAD ENOUGH COUGAR PROBLEMS AND CALLED IN THE DOGS! FORTUNATE FOR BIG CAT, THEY HAD ARRIVED AT DUSK AND THE DOG OWNERS WERE WAITING FOR DAYBREAK TO LET THE DOGS LOOSE ON HIS TRAIL.

CHAPTER 10

CHASED AGAIN!

BIG CAT'S DISTASTE FOR DOGS MADE HIM TURN QUICKLY AND LOPE AWAY. KNOWING THAT HE HAD TO GET AS FAR AWAY AS POSSIBLE HE RAN TOWARDS THE LAKE THAT HE HAD PASSED EARLIER. STOPPING TO LAP SOME WATER HE DRANK DEEPLY. PAST EXPERIENCE TOLD HIM THAT HE WOULD NEED AS MUCH CLEAN WATER AS HE COULD DRINK. WORKING HIS WAY AROUND THE LAKE, HE SUPRISED FROGS AS THEY LEAPT INTO THE WATER AND A MUSKRAT THAT SCURRIED AWAY.

PUSHING HIMSELF; HE TROTTED ALONG MAKING DISTANCE BETWEEN HIMSELF AND THE DOGS AS HE RAN INTO THE WIND WHICH HAPPENED TO BE IN A SOUTHERLY DIRECTION. COMING UPON A RIVER, HE SEARCHED FOR A SHALLOW CROSSING AND WADED OUT INTO THE WATER BUT SUDDENLY HE WAS SWIMMING AS THE RIVER BOTTOM DROPPED OFF.

SWIMMING WITH STRONG STROKES; HE TRAVELED FAR DOWN THE RIVER BEFORE HE WAS ABLE TO CLIMB UP THE OTHER RIVER BANK. ONLY AFTER STRUGGLING FOR SOME TIME TRYING TO GET A GOOD FOOT-HOLD WAS HE ABLE TO DRAG HIMSELF OUT OF THE RIVER. LUCKY FOR BIG CAT; THIS SWIMMING ADVENTURE SAVED HIM FROM FURTHER PURSUIT BY THE DOGS!

ALTHOUGH THE TRACKING DOGS SEARCHED IN VAIN FOR BIG CATS TRIAL ALONG THE RIVER BED; THEY WEREN'T ABLE TO FIND HIS SCENT AND WERE PULLED BACK BY THEIR OWNERS AS DARKNESS APPROACHED. CROSSING OPEN FIELDS UNDER THE COVER OF NIGHT; BIG CAT RAN AS STRAIGHT AWAY FROM THE CHASE AS HE COULD. SOMETIMES; HAVING TO COME CLOSE TO HOMES HE

SNUCK BY AS SILENTLY AS POSSIBLE AND WHEN HE SURPRISED DOGS, HE QUICKLY RAN AWAY FROM THEM.

TRAVELING INTO THE WIND FOR MANY MILES; BIG CAT HAD ALL KINDS OF ODORS PASS BY HIS NOSE. BUT ONE NEW, UNIQUE ODOR STOPPED HIM IN HIS TRACKS! SLOWLY APPROACHING A DOG HOUSE, HE COULD SMELL THE ODOR OF NEWBORN PUPPIES. THE MOTHER DOG GROWLED; AS SHE SENSED DANGER APPROACHING HER DOG HOUSE. BIG CATS NATURAL INSTINCT WAS TO TAKE ADVANTAGE OF THE SITUATION AND ELIMINATE THE ENEMY BUT THE CLOSE PROXIMITY OF HUMANS KEPT HIM FROM APPROACHING ANY CLOSER AS THE DOG HOUSE WAS VERY NEAR THE HUMAN'S HOUSE. BIG CAT TURNED AND CONTINUED ON HIS WAY.

AFTER TRAVELING IN OPEN COUNTRY FOR SOMETIME; BIG CAT WELCOMED THE GROUP OF TREES AHEAD OF HIM AND ENTERED THE TREES HOPING TO FIND SOMETHING TO EAT. HE HADN'T EATEN FOR A COUPLE DAYS SO HE STARTED SEARCHING EAGERLY, FOR A MEAL AS HE WAS FEELING MORE AT EASE AND UNHURRIED.

AS HE SEARCHED FOR FOOD NUMEROUS ODORS ENTERED HIS NOSE AND AS HE WAS DRAWN TO THE MANY SCENTS, HE NOTICED A LITTLE RED LIGHT ON A BLACK OBJECT ATTACHED TO A TREE WITH A PILE OF GRAIN AND OTHER SUBSTANCES INCLUDING VARIOUS MEATS BELOW IT ON THE GROUND. WALKING UP TO THE PILE, HE SNIFFED IT AND COULD SMELL SWEET POTATOES AND SCENTS OF MEAT AND OTHER FOODS.

BEING AS HUNGRY AS HE WAS, HE GRABBED A MOUTHFUL AND BEGAN TO EAT. WHAT HE DIDN'T REALIZE WAS THAT HIS PICTURE WAS BEING TAKEN BY A TRAIL CAMERA OF A BEAR HUNTER AND THE HUNTER WAS SURPRISED TO SEE PICTURES OF BIG CATS ON HIS TRAIL CAMERA LATER.

DAYLIGHT WAS BEGINNING TO CREEP INTO THE WOODS AS HE FINISHED EATING WHAT HE WANTED FROM THE PILE; SO HE STARTED TO EXPLORE THE WOODED AREA FOR A PLACE TO REST. BIG CAT BEGAN TO LOOK FOR SHELTER AS THE COMING DAYLIGHT REMINDED HIM TO FIND A PLACE TO REST FOR THE DAY. AS HE SEARCHED THROUGH THE WOODED PLOT; BIG CAT CHECKED OUT A LEANING TREE WITH HANGING BRANCHES BUT HE DIDN'T FEEL SAFE RESTING UNDER IT, SO HE CONTINUED LOOKING.

MOST OF THE WOODS WERE TALL POPLAR TREES (ALSO KNOWN AS ASPEN TREES) WITH LITTLE OR NO LIMBS WITH AN OCCASIONAL OAK TREE BUT HE FINALLY FOUND A LARGE WHITE PINE WITH BIG BRANCHES. AS HE LOOKED UP THE TREE HE SAW A POSSIBLE SAFE PLACE TO HIDE AND REST FOR THE DAY. LUCKY FOR BIG CAT, THE TOP OF THE TREE HAD BEEN HIT BY LIGHTNING AND AFTER BREAKING OFF AND PARTIALLY ROTTING OVER TIME, THERE WAS A BIG HOLLOW AREA IN THE TREE.

LEAPING UPWARDS, HIS CLAWS SUNK INTO THE BARK AND ONE PAW WRAPPED AROUND A SMALL BRANCH. THIS GAVE HIM A BETTER HOLD AND HE CLAWED HIS WAY UP THE TREE USING BRANCHES TO SUPPORT HIMSELF. REACHING THE HOLLOWED AREA, HE CLAWED A FEW CLUMPS OF ROTTED WOOD OUT OF THE WAY AND STEPPED INTO THE OPENING. IT SANK A LITTLE UNDER HIS FEET BUT SEEMED SAFE ENOUGH TO HIM FOR A BED. AS MOST CATS DO, HE CIRCLED A COUPLE OF TIMES IN THE ENCLOSURE THEN CURLED UP TO REST.

CHAPTER 11

MORE DREAMS AND A BUCK

DRIFTING OFF TO SLEEP, BIG CAT'S MEMORIES WENT BACK TO THE BLACK HILLS WHERE HE WAS BORN. IN HIS DREAM HE WAS HUNTING FOR FOOD AND AFTER SEEING A MOVEMENT IN THE SAND IN FRONT OF HIM HIS ATTENTION WAS DRAWN IN THAT DIRECTION. IT WAS A RATTLE SNAKE AND THOUGH HE KNEW IT WAS DANGEROUS TO ADVANCE; HIS CURIOSITY AND HUNGER OVER-RULED HIS LOGIC AND HE MOVED IN FOR THE KILL.

THE SNAKE WATCHED HIM IN A COILED, STRIKING POSITION AS BIG CAT CIRCLED HIM. AS HE STEPPED CLOSER TO THE SNAKE IT STRUCK OUT AT HIM AND HE JUMPED BACKWARDS, JUST QUICK ENOUGH TO KEEP FROM GETTING BITTEN BY THE SNAKE. THIS CONTINUED AS BIG CAT KEPT CIRCLING THE SNAKE WITH THE SNAKE STRIKING AND HE JUMPING BACKWARDS.

THE NEXT MOMENT, THE DREAMED CHANGED AND A HAWK WAS ON THE SNAKE WITH ITS CLAWS STUCK IN THE SNAKE. THE HAWK HAD KILLED THE SNAKE AND BIG CAT CHARGED IN AND POUNCED ON THE HAWK BEFORE IT COULD FLY AWAY . . . DRIFTING OFF AS DREAMS OFTEN DO; THE DREAM CHANGED AGAIN TO THE OPEN, SANDY SOIL OF HIS HOMELAND. HE HAD EATEN AND WAS FEELING CONTENT AS HE LAY ON A LEDGE OVER-LOOKING VAST, DRY LANDS WITH BUTTES THAT CASCADED UPWARDS TO THE SKY.

SUDDENLY, A NOISE FROM THE FOREST BELOW HIM WOKE HIM ABRUPTLY FROM HIS SLEEP! AS HE LOOKED DOWN FROM THE TREE HE COULD SEE SOME WHITETAIL DEER WERE WALKING TOWARDS THE FIELD THAT WAS JUST A SHORT DISTANCE AWAY FROM THE TREE THAT HE WAS IN. NOTICING THAT IT WAS

BEGINNING TO GET DARK; BIG CAT STEPPED OUT OF THE HOLLOW TREE ONTO A LIMB AND WATCHED THE DEER BELOW IN THE LOW LIGHT OF THE EVENING. A DOE AND FAWN HAD PASSED AT A DISTANCE AND ANOTHER DOE FOLLOWED.

WATCHING THE DEER WALK AWAY HE WAITED UNTIL THEY WERE OUT OF HEARING THEN LOWERED HIMSELF DOWN THE TREE TAIL FIRST. HIS CLAWS DUG INTO THE BARK AND PIECES OF BARK FELL TO THE GROUND AS HE CLIMBED DOWN.

REACHING THE GROUND; HE CAREFULLY SCANNED THE WOODS AND INHALED THE SCENTS TO MAKE SURE ALL WAS OK TO BEGIN HIS STALKING OF THE DEER. THE ONLY SCENT HE COULD SMELL WAS THAT OF DEER; SO HE PROCEEDED CAUTIOUSLY FORWARD FOLLOWING THE TRAIL OF THE DEER TOWARDS THE FIELD.

CROUCHING LOW; BIG CAT MOVED WITH, ALMOST TOTAL SILENCE, AS HE STALKED THE DEER. AFTER STALKING FOR ABOUT A HUNDRED YARDS; HE CAME TO THE EDGE OF THE ALFALFA FIELD WHERE THE DEER WERE FEEDING. THICK BRUSH CAME RIGHT UP TO THE EDGE OF THE FIELD SO; BIG CAT WAS ABLE TO STAY HIDDEN OUT OF SIGHT OF THE DEER IN THE FIELD. THE WIND HAD SHIFTED AND BIG CAT'S INSTINCT TOLD HIM TO APPROACH DOWNWIND OF THE DEER SO THAT THE DEER WOULD NOT BE ABLE TO SMELL HIM.

TURNING TOWARDS THE BREEZE, HE LEFT THE DEER TRAIL AND CAREFULLY WORKED HIS WAY AROUND BRUSH, STEPPING OVER FALLEN BRANCHES AND FOUND A BIG TREE THAT HAD BEEN BLOWN DOWN BY THE WIND. THE ROOTS STUCK UP IN THE AIR ON THE BOTTOM OF THE FALLEN OAK TREE AND A LARGE CLUMP OF DIRT CLUNG TO THEM. BIG CAT JUMPED UP ON THE FALLEN TREE IN ORDER TO BE ELEVATED ENOUGH TO GET A BETTER VIEW. HE HAD JUST JUMPED UP ON THE TRUNK OF THE TREE WHEN HE HEARD A SOUND OFF TO HIS RIGHT.

LOWERING HIS BODY TO A CROUCH, BIG CAT WAITED. THERE WAS SILENCE FOR A WHILE BUT THEN HE SAW MOVEMENT AS SOMETHING WAS COMING HIS DIRECTION. THE BRUSH WAS FAIRLY THICK AROUND HIM BUT HE CAUGHT GLIMPSES OF WHAT APPEARED TO BE A DEER. PEERING SILENTLY THROUGH THE BRUSH; BIG CAT COULD SEE THAT THE APPROACHING DEER WAS COMING ON THE TRAIL THAT WOULD BRING THE DEER RIGHT PAST HIM.

THE WIND WAS STILL IN BIG CAT'S FAVOR AS THE UNSUSPECTING DEER APPROACHED HIM. AS THE DEER DREW NEARER, BIG CAT SAW THAT IT WAS A GOOD-SIZED BUCK WITH HIS HEAD DOWN TO THE GROUND SNIFFING THE TRAIL. APPARENTLY, THE BUCK WAS IN "RUT" AND FOLLOWING A DOE'S SCENT.

GENERALLY, BIG CAT FAVORED FAWNS OR DOES BUT THE BUCK WAS TOO INVITING TO PASS UP. AS THE BUCK DREW NEARER, ADRENALIN PUMPED INTO BIG CAT'S BLOOD VEINS IN ANTICIPATION! JUST AS THE BUCK WAS ABOUT TO PASS BY, HE SPOTTED BIG CAT ON THE TREE. JUMPING SIDEWAYS AWAY FROM BIG CAT, HE STUMBLED IN THE BRUSH FOR A SECOND. AT THAT MOMENT, BIG CAT SPRANG WITH ALL HIS MIGHT AND MANAGED TO SINK HIS CLAWS INTO THE SIDE OF THE BUCK WITH ONE PAW OVER THE BACK OF THE BUCK. STRUGGLING TO GET AWAY, THE BUCK DRAGGED BIG CAT INTO THE FIELD WITH HIM.

AS SOON AS BIG CAT HAD HIS CHANCE, HE LUNGED FORWARD SINKING HIS TEETH INTO THE BUCK'S NECK. THIS SLOWED THE BUCK DOWN BUT HE WAS STILL ON HIS FEET WITH BIG CAT HANGING ONTO HIM. TIRING, THE BUCK STOPPED AND JUST STOOD THERE WITH BIG CAT HANGING ON HIS SIDE. BIG CAT WASN'T ABOUT TO GIVE UP HIS CATCH AND CLUNG TO THE BUCKS THROAT. MINUTES DRAGGED BY AS THE BUCK BEGAN TO WEAKEN. FINALLY; THE BUCK BEGAN TO STAGGER AND BIG CAT SAW HIS CHANCE.

BRACING HIS FEET UNDER HIMSELF, BIG CAT KNOCKED THE BUCK OFF BALANCE AND THE BUCK LANDED ON HIS SIDE WITH BIG CAT HOLDING HIM DOWN. THE BIG CAT HELD THE BUCKS HEAD WITH HIS PAWS TO KEEP FROM BEING INJURED BY HIS ANTLERS. HOWEVER, IN THIS POSITION THE BUCK WAS ABLE TO KICK AT BIG CAT WITH HIS HIND LEGS AND COULD INJURE HIM HARM. BIG CAT STRUGGLED TO STAY AWAY FROM THE KICKING HIND–LEGS BUT WAS STILL BEING HIT BY THEM, OCCASIONALLY.

HE KNEW HE HAD TO CHANGE POSITIONS TO KEEP FROM BEING TORN OPEN BY THE BUCK'S SHARP HOOFS OR LET THE BUCK GO. WITH ONE SWIFT MOVE, BIG CAT RELEASED THE HOLD ON THE BUCK'S NECK AND QUICKLY SWUNG HIS BODY OVER THE BUCK LANDING AWAY FROM THE KICKING HOOFS. THEN, GRASPING THE BUCKS NOSE IN HIS MOUTH; HE PULLED THE HEAD SIDEWAYS AS HE DUG HIS CLAWS INTO THE BUCKS SHOULDER HOLDING HIM DOWN. HE WAS NOW ON THE TOP SIDE OF THE BUCK AWAY FROM HIS FEET.

ALTHOUGH, THE BUCK CONTINUED TO KICK AT BIG CAT, HE WASN'T ABLE TO REACH BIG CAT OR GET HIS FEET UNDER HIMSELF ENOUGH TO STAND UP. THE COMMOTION HAD CAUSED SUCH A STIR WITH THE OTHER DEER THAT *ANOTHER BUCK*, ACTUALLY, RAN UP TO HELP HIS FELLOW BUCK, THEN DECIDED HE BETTER GET OUT OF THERE! BIG CAT COULD TELL THAT THE BUCK WAS GETTING WEAKER

AS HIS STRUGGLING BECAME LESS FORCEFUL. THAT WAS GOOD FOR BIG CAT SINCE HE WAS BEGINNING TO FEEL EXHAUSTED HIMSELF.

WHEN IT WAS OVER, BIG CAT PANTED AND LOOKED AROUND WHILE HOLDING THE DEAD DEER. THEN GRABBING THE BUCK BY HIS NECK, BIG CAT STRADDLED HIM AND BEGAN DRAGGING HIM ACROSS THE FIELD TOWARDS THE WOODS. HIS MUSCLES STRAINED AS HE PARTIALLY LIFTED THE BUCK AND STAGGERED BACK AND FORTH, SLOWLY MAKING HEADWAY WITH THE BUCK DRAGGING BETWEEN HIS LEGS. THE HORNS WERE A PROBLEM AS THEY BUMPED AGAINST BIG CAT AS HE DRAGGED THE BUCK. CHANGING HIS GRIP, BIG CAT SUNK HIS TEETH INTO THE BASE OF THE BUCK'S HEAD AND CONTINUED FORWARD. THIS WORKED BETTER BECAUSE BIG CAT COULD STEADY THE HEAD OF THE BUCK AS HE WENT ALONG WITHOUT BEING BUMPED BY THE HORNS.

FINALLY, REACHING THE BRUSH, BIG CAT RESTED AGAIN BEFORE ATTEMPTING THE HARDER BATTLE OF GETTING THE BUCK THROUGH THE BRUSH INTO A SAFE HIDING PLACE. SNIFFED THE AIR TO CHECK FOR DANGER, BIG CAT BEGAN PULLING THE BUCK INTO THE HEAVY BRUSH WHICH MADE THE PROCESS OF DRAGGING THE BUCK MUCH MORE DIFFICULT. SO LETTING GO OF THE BUCK, BIG CAT TURNED AROUND AND GRABBED THE BUCK SO THAT HE COULD PULL IT BACKWARDS AS THE BRUSH CLUNG TO THE HORNS AND LEGS.

THIS PROCESS OF DRAGGING THE BUCK THROUGH THE BRUSH WAS SLOW GOING AND BIG CAT COULD ONLY DRAG THE BUCK A FEW FEET BEFORE RESTING. AFTER DRAGGING THE BUCK FOR ABOUT ONE HUNDRED AND FIFTY YARDS INTO THE WOODS; BIG CAT FELT SECURE ENOUGH TO SETTLE DOWN TO HIS MEAL. HE FINALLY HAD ENOUGH FOOD SO HE DIDN'T HAVE TO WORRY ABOUT A MEAL FOR A GOOD WEEK.

AFTER FEASTING AND KEEPING A KEEN WATCH FOR OTHER PREDATORS AND MAN, BIG CAT LICKED HIMSELF CLEAN. INSTINCT TOLD HIM TO HIDE HIS KILL FROM OTHER PREDATORS SO, DRAGGING THE BUCK TO A SECLUDED SPOT NEAR HIS TREE THAT HE HAD SLEPT IN HE BEGAN TO BURY IT. STRADDLING THE BUCK, BIG CAT DUG HIS CLAWS INTO THE DEBRIS AND PULLED THE LEAVES AND STICKS OVER THE BUCK. HE CHANGED POSITIONS AND CONTINUED THE PROCESS UNTIL HE FELT THE BUCK WAS COMPLETELY COVERED.

THEN, AFTER CHECKING AND SNIFFING THE PILE TO SATISFY HIMSELF THAT THE BUCK WAS HIDDEN WELL ENOUGH; HE TURNED AND LEAPT UP THE TREE CLIMBING UP TO HIS HOLLOW BED IN THE TREE AND SETTLED DOWN TO REST.

CHAPTER 12

SCAVENGERS

A SOUND BELOW HIM WOKE BIG CAT AND LOOKING DOWN HE SAW COYOTES CHECKING OUT THE AREA FOR A MEAL. THEIR NOSES TOLD THEM A FRESH KILL WAS NEAR. IT WAS STARTING TO GET DARK AND OTHER PREDATORS WERE LOOKING FOR A FREE SUPPER. BIG CAT STEPPED OUT INTO THE VIEW OF THE COYOTES AND LET OUT A GROWL. THE COYOTES STOPPED IN THEIR TRACKS AND LOOKED AROUND FOR THE DANGER. AT FIRST, THEY COULDN'T TELL WHERE THE GROWL HAD COME FROM BUT WHEN BIG CAT LET OUT A LOUDER GROWL THEY SAW HIM IN THE TREE. THEY STOOD THEIR GROUND SEEING THAT THE MOUNTAIN LION WAS HIGH IN A TREE, SO BIG CAT BEGAN TO CLIMB DOWN THE TREE, GROWLING AS HE DID.

THE COYOTES DIDN'T NEED ANY FURTHER PERSUASION AND DISAPPEARED INTO THE FOREST. WHEN BIG CAT REACHED THE GROUND, HE WENT STRAIGHT TO HIS BUCK TO CHECK IT OUT. FORTUNATELY, THE COYOTES HADN'T FOUND IT AND IT WAS AS HE LEFT IT. CHECKING THE AREA FOR ANY FURTHER INTRUDERS; HE CLEANED A SPOT OF DEBRIS OFF THE BUCK SO THAT HE COULD SETTLE DOWN AND EAT SOME MORE.

AFTER GETTING HIS FILL; HE SAT ON HIS HUNCHES AND LICKED HIMSELF CLEAN. MUCH LIKE HOUSE CATS; COUGARS ARE PRIMING ANIMALS AND THEY KEEP THEMSELVES AS CLEAN AS POSSIBLE. AFTER COVERING HIS MEAL AND FEELING SECURE ABOUT HIS SITUATION OF HAVING PLENTY OF FOOD TO EAT; BIG CAT CLIMBED UP THE TREE AND SETTLED DOWN TO REST AGAIN.

A FEW HOURS LATER; ANOTHER NOISE BELOW HIM DISTURBED HIS PEACEFUL REST. GETTING UP AND LOOKING DOWN TO THE GROUND, BIG CAT COULD SEE MORE VARMINTS GOING AFTER HIS HIDDEN PRIZE, THIS TIME A FAMILY OF RACCOONS WERE DIGGING AT HIS BUCK TRYING TO REMOVE THE COVERING AND GRABBING BITS OF MEAT.

BIG CAT LET OUT A GROWL AND STARTED TO CLIMB DOWN. THE RACCOONS DIDN'T EVEN DEBATE THE SITUATION AS THEY HEADED OUT OF THERE IN ALL DIRECTIONS! AFTER CHECKING OUT HIS DEER REMAINS, BIG CAT WASN'T FEELING AS SECURE ABOUT HIS KILL AS BEFORE AND GETTING A GOOD HOLD OF IT HE STARTED TO DRAG IT SOMEWHERE ELSE. NOT READY TO GIVE UP HIS KILL, HE HAD TO FIND A BETTER HIDING PLACE.

AS HE PULLED THE CARCASS, STICKS, DIRT AND LEAVES CLUNG TO IT WHICH MADE IT MORE DIFFICULT TO MOVE. BIG CAT DIDN'T LET THAT SLOW HIM DOWN AS HE CONTINUED TO DRAG IT TO A SAFER PLACE. AFTER ABOUT SEVENTY FIVE YARDS HE STOPPED AND SURVEYED THE AREA FOR A GOOD HIDING PLACE. SEEING A THICK CLUMP OF BRUSH AND DEBRIS, HE BEGAN TO DRAG THE DEER TO IT. FINDING A BARE SPOT OF GROUND IN THE THICKET, HE BEGAN TO CLAW AT THE SOFT SOIL AND STARTED DIGGING A HOLE.

AFTER PAWING AND DIGGING FOR SOME TIME, BIG CAT WAS ABLE TO DIG A TRENCH DEEP ENOUGH TO DRAG THE CARCASS OF THE DEER INTO IT. PULLING THE BUCK INTO THE HOLE TOOK SOME EFFORT AS HE HAD TO DRAG IT THROUGH BRUSH AND BRANCHES. THEN GETTING THE DEER INTO PLACE, BIG CAT STOOD OVER IT AND BEGAN TO PULL DIRT, LEAVES AND DEBRIS ON TOP OF IT AGAIN, FIRST IN ONE DIRECTION THEN IN ANOTHER UNTIL HE FELT SATISFIED THAT IT WAS HIDDEN. THIS NEW HIDING SPOT WAS NEAR HIS HOLLOW TREE SO; AFTER LOOKING AROUND TO SEE IF ALL WAS SAFE AND SECURE HE CLIMBED HIS TREE AND SETTLED DOWN TO REST.

AS TO BE EXPECTED, BIG CAT DIDN'T GET MUCH REST BEFORE MORE MEAT-EATERS WERE AFTER HIS KILL. THIS TIME; BIG CAT WOKE UP TO SEE A YOUNG BEAR DIGGING AT THE DEBRIS OVER HIS BUCK AFTER IT HAD PICKED UP THE SCENT OF HIS KILL. GROWLING AT THE BEAR DIDN'T CHASE IT AWAY, SO BIG CAT HAD TO DEFEND IT.

THE BEAR CONTINUED TO CHEW AT THE BUCK AS BIG CAT CLIMBED DOWN THE TREE; ONLY GLANCING AT BIG CAT ONCE AND AWHILE WHILE HE ATE. THE

BEAR WAITED UNTIL BIG CAT WAS ALMOST UPON HIM BEFORE IT TURNED AND GRUNTED AT HIM. THE CHALLENGE WAS ON AND SOMEONE HAD TO GIVE IN!

BIG CAT GROWLED FURIOUSLY AND TOOK A MENACING STEP TOWARDS THE BEAR TRYING TO BE AS THREATENING AS HE COULD AS THE BEAR RAISED HIMSELF UP ON HIS HIND LEGS GROWLING BACK AS BIG CAT CIRCLED HIM. BIG CAT REMEMBERED HIS ENCOUNTER WITH THE GRIZZLY WHEN HE WAS YOUNGER BUT THIS BEAR WAS MUCH SMALLER AND *HE WASN'T GOING TO GIVE IN!*

SNARLING AND GRUNTING THE ANIMALS *EYED EACH OTHER* LOOKING FOR THE OTHERS WEAKNESS. BIG CAT RAISED HIS RIGHT FRONT PAW AND SLASHED AT THE BEAR. THE BEAR CONTINUED TO MAKE HIS THREATENING SOUNDS WHICH VARY FROM A GRUNT TO A GROAN-LIKE HOWL AS HE DODGED BACK AND FORTH.

SNARLING FURIOUSLY; BIG CAT CLOSED IN ON THE BEAR AND BATTED AT HIM WITH HIS FRONT PAWS WITHHOLDING HIS CLAWS NOT TO SERIOUSLY HARM THE BEAR BUT WANTING TO DRIVE HIM AWAY. THE BEAR WAS INTIMIDATED AND BEGAN TO BACK AWAY. BIG CAT SAW HIS CHANCE AND CONTINUED TO GROWL AND SLASH AT THE BEAR AS THE BEAR RETREATED. THE YOUNG BEAR SENSED THAT HE WAS "OVER-POWERED" SO HE TURNED AND STARTED RUNNING AWAY. BIG CAT PURSUED HIM AND DIDN'T STOP CHASING UNTIL HE FELT THE BEAR WAS FAR ENOUGH AWAY FROM HIS KILL FOR HIM TO FEEL IT WAS SAFE.

BECAUSE *ALL* THESE MARAUDERS HAD FOUND HIS DEER, BIG CAT KNEW HE HAD TO GET HIS KILL INTO A SAFER SPOT. SENSING THAT THE SCAVENGERS WOULD RETURN, HE BEGAN SEARCHING FOR A SAFER PLACE TO HIDE HIS KILL. EYEING A BIG OAK TREE WITH SOME LARGE BRANCHES SPREADING OUT FROM THE TRUNK, BIG CAT GRABBED THE BUCK BY THE BASE OF THE SKULL AND DRUG IT TOWARDS THE OAK TREE.

AS BIG CAT DRUG THE BUCK ALONG, IT STILL WASN'T EASY TO MOVE BUT HE WAS GRATEFUL THAT IT WASN'T AS HEAVY AS WHEN HE FIRST GOT IT. WHEN HE REACHED THE TREE HE LOOKED UP TO STUDY THE BEST WAY FOR HIM TO GET THE DEER UP THE TREE. CIRCLING TO THE OTHER SIDE HE SAW A BRANCH CLOSER TO THE GROUND THEN THE OTHERS AND PROCEEDED TO PULL THE BUCK AROUND THE TREE.

GETTING A FIRM HOLD OF THE DEER HE CROUCHED AS LOW AS POSSIBLE AND USING EVERY MUSCLE IN HIS BODY, HE LUNGED UP THE TREE DIGGING INTO THE BARK WITH HIS LONG CLAWS. EVERY INCH HE WENT UP THE TREE TOOK

GREAT EFFORT AND STRENGTH AS HE PULLED BOTH HIMSELF AND THE BUCK HIGHER. BARK FELL IN CHUNKS AS HE DUG HIS CLAWS INTO THE TREE BARK AND STRUGGLED UPWARD WITH THE BUCK'S HORNS CATCHING ON SMALL BRANCHES.

REACHING THE FIRST BIG BRANCH HE STRAINED TO GET ENOUGH OF THE DEER OVER IT SO THAT IT WOULD BALANCE THERE. FINALLY, GETTING THE BUCK TO BALANCE ON THE LIMB, HE STOPPED ON THE BRANCH HOLDING THE DEER IN PLACE WITH HIS BIG PAWS AND RESTED.

CATCHING HIS BREATH, BIG CAT LOOKED BELOW AND CHECKED FOR ANY VARMINTS OR APPROACHING DANGERS. SENSING THAT HE NEEDED TO CLIMB HIGHER UP THE TREE TO PROTECT HIS CATCH, HE BEGAN PULLING THE BUCK UP TO FIND A BETTER PLACE TO HIDE HIS MEAL. SEEING THAT THERE WAS A FORK ABOUT TWELVE FEET ABOUT HIM IN THE TREE, HE PROCEEDED ON UP THE TREE.

KNOWING THAT THE SPLIT IN THE TREE WOULD BE A GOOD PLACE TO HIDE HIS BOUNTY, HE CONTINUED PULLING THE BUCK UP, WRAPPING HIS STRONG FRONT LEGS AROUND THE OAK TREE. THE DEAD WEIGHT OF THE BUCK DRAINED HIS STRENGTH BUT HE WAS FINALLY ABLE TO PULL IT INTO THE FORK OF THE TREE.

FEELING THE RELIEF OF GETTING HIS DEER OUT OF THE REACH OF THE MARAUDERS; BIG CAT SAT PANTING WITH HIS TONGUE HANGING OUT BEFORE RELAXING AND STARTING TO EAT. HIS CATCH NOW SECURE IN HIS CLUTCHES, HE SETTLED INTO A COMFORTABLE POSITION AND ENJOYED THE TEMPORARY PEACE.

CHAPTER 13

STILL SEARCHING AND A HORSE

AFTER SPENDING ABOUT A WEEK SLEEPING AND EATING FROM HIS BUCK, BIG CAT KNEW THAT IT WAS TIME TO CONTINUE ON HIS JOURNEY. AFTER EATING MOST OF THE DEER ALL THAT WAS LEFT WERE A FEW BONES AND HIDE AND THE SCAVENGER LIKE VULTURES, CROWS AND A VARIETY OF OTHER CREATURES WERE GATHERING BELOW EATING THE FALLEN SCRAPS.

ALL THE *UNWANTED* VARMINTS HAD BIG CAT IRRITATED AND ONLY HURRIED HIS DECISION TO MOVE ON. AFTER THE RACCOONS HAD RETURNED AND SNIFFED AROUND THE BASE OF THE TREE EATING FALLEN MORSELS AND THE CROWS HAD FOUND SCRAPS AND SAT CAWING AT HIM IN NEARBY TREES, BIG CAT HAD HAD ENOUGH!

AT DUSK, HE WORKED HIS WAY DOWN THE TREE AND HEADED IN A SOUTH-EASTERN DIRECTION TRAVELING INTO THE WIND LEAVING PARTS OF THE SKELETON IN THE TREE LIMBS. WALKING OUT ONTO THE FIELD WHERE HE HAD TAKEN THE BUCK, HE STARTLED A COUPLE DOES AND FAWNS ON THE OTHER SIDE OF THE FIELD. AS THE DEER SNORTED A WARNING AND RAISED THEIR TAILS AND RAN OFF THE FIELD; BIG CAT HARDLY NOTICED AS HE CONTINUED ON HIS WAY.

BIG CAT HAD GONE MANY MILES SINCE THE DOG CHASING DAYS IN WASHBURN COUNTY AND HAD ENTERED INTO PEPIN COUNTY NORTH OF EAU CLAIRE. FORTUNATELY, NO ONE HERE HAD GATHERED DOGS TO CHASE HIM AND HE WAS STARTING TO FEEL MORE RELAXED. AS BIG CAT TRAVELED THROUGH THE COUNTRY SIDE HE CAME ACROSS MANY DIFFERENT SCENTS TO INVESTIGATE.

ONE PARTICULAR SCENT FROM A SMALL CLUMP OF TREES IN A FIELD DREW HIM NEAR. HONING IN ON THE SCENT, BIG CAT WALKED UP TO IT TO CHECK IT OUT AND THE ODOR TOLD HIM IT WAS A BOBCAT SCENTING ROCK. HE TURNED AND LEFT HIS OWN SCENT ON THE SPOT BY LIFTING HIS TAIL AND SQUIRTING. HE WAS THE "BOSS" NOW AND THE BOBCAT BETTER RESPECT THAT!

APPROACHING A FARM LATE ONE NIGHT, HE CAUTIOUSLY INSPECTED THE BARNYARD TAKING IN THE SCENTS OF CATTLE AND OTHER FARM CREATURES AS HE KEPT HIS EYES AND EARS OPEN FOR ANY DOGS. KNOWING THAT ONLY TROUBLE WOULD COME IF HE STAYED AROUND THE FARM, BIG CAT KEPT TRAVELING. THE NEXT MORNING THE FARMER AND HIS SON FIRST THOUGHT THAT A BEAR HAD PASSED BY BUT AFTER CLOSER OBSERVATION AND THE HELP OF A BIOLOGIST FROM THE DNR, THEY ASCERTAINED THAT IT WAS A MOUNTAIN LION AND THEY HOPED TO FIND MORE EVIDENCE ABOUT THE CAT.

THE DNR HAS ALSO, OFFERED THE FOLLOWING PUBLIC INFORMATION ABOUT COUGARS ON THE INTERNET. MALE MOUNTAIN LIONS ARE BETWEEN 80 TO 95 INCHES IN LENGTH—(ONE INCH LESS THAN 8 FEET LONG!) FEMALES BEING SLIGHTLY SMALLER, MEASURE BETWEEN 72 AND 80 INCHES.

THEIR LONG ROPE-LIKE TAILS ARE BETWEEN 28 TO 38 INCHES IN LENGTH AND AN ADULT COUGAR CAN STAND AS TALL AS 31 INCHES HIGH—(ONLY 5 INCHES UNDER 3 FEET AT THE SHOULDERS!) THEIR PAW PRINTS ARE WIDER THAN THEY ARE LONG FROM 2.7 TO 4 INCHES IN LENGTH AND 2.8 TO 4.5 INCHES WIDE. WHEN THEY WALK THEIR CLAWS DO NOT SHOW AS THEY ARE RETRACTED INTO THEIR PAWS.

TO PROTECT THEIR PRINTS FOR FURTHER OBSERVATION THE DNR ALSO SUGGESTS PUTTING AN INVERTED PAIL OVER THEM UNTIL THEY CAN BE CHECKED BY A PROFESSIONAL. IN THE PAST YEARS THE DNR HAS EXPERIMENTED WITH "HAIR SNARES" ON RUBBING POSTS BAITED WITH CAT LURE TO OBTAIN DNA SAMPLES OF COUGARS.

IT SEEMS THEY HAVE EVEN DONE TRIALS ON CAPTIVE ANIMALS TO SEE WHICH FORMULA GETS THE BEST REACTION. IN THE WILD, THEIR EFFORTS TO SNARE MOUNTAIN LION HAIRS HAD GOTTEN THEM SAMPLES OF BOBCAT AND BEAR HAIRS, PLUS UNKNOWN MATERIALS AT THE TIME OF TESTING IN 2006.

AFTER WALKING PAST THE FARM, BIG CAT CROSSED FIELDS OF CORN AND SOYBEANS THE MOST PLENTIFUL CROPS OF THE FARM LANDS. HE CAME ACROSS

SMALL WOODED CLUMPS OF TREES FOR SHELTER BUT SINCE HE WAS ENTERING INTO A MORE POPULATED AREA HE HAD TO HIDE FROM PASSING CAR LIGHTS MORE AND MORE OFTEN BY DODGING BEHIND TURNED-UP TREE ROOTS AND ANYTHING NEARBY. THE LACK OF COVER AND THE PRESENCE OF MORE PEOPLE MADE BIG CAT FEEL UNEASY IN HIS TRAVELING.

ATTEMPTING TO STAY CLEAR OF HUMANS WAS BECOMING MORE OF A CHALLENGE AS HE TRAVELED SOUTH BECAUSE OF APPROACHING CITIES AND TOWNS SO; BIG CAT CHOSE AN EASTERLY DIRECTION. HE ONLY FOUND SHELTER DURING THE DAY IN SOME OF THOSE RARE WOODED AREAS AND OFTEN WAS ALMOST DISCOVERED BY FARMERS DOING THEIR FIELD WORK AS THEY PASSED CLOSE BY HIM.

ALL THE HEAVY CONGESTION OF PEOPLE AND THEIR NUMEROUS ROADS MADE HIM NERVOUS AS HE TRAVELED CAREFULLY THROUGH THE AREA TRYING TO KEEP OUT OF SIGHT OF HUMANS. ONE NIGHT HE HAD TO CROSS A FREEWAY OF TRAFFIC TO CONTINUE HIS JOURNEY. AFTER LEAPING THE FENCE BY THE INTERSTATE HE REALIZED THE CARS WERE NOT LETTING UP AND HE WAS GETTING ANXIOUS ABOUT CROSSING THE HIGHWAY.

AFTER PACING BACK AND FORTH WAITING FOR THE TRAFFIC TO LESSEN; HE FINALLY HAD HIS CHANCE WHEN HE NOTICED THAT THE STEADY TRAFFIC AND NOISE HAD LESSONED. LEAPING OUT OF THE BRUSH HE RACED DOWN THE FREEWAY BANK HEADING FOR THE OTHER SIDE. HE WAS JUST CROSSING THE FIRST LANE WHEN HE SAW HEADLIGHTS COMING DOWN THE OTHER LANE TOWARDS HIM.

ADRENALIN POURED INTO HIS VEINS AS HE RACED UP THE OTHER SIDE AND OVER THE FENCE WITH THE CAR LIGHTS CATCHING HIM IN THERE BEAMS. THE PEOPLE IN THE APPROACHING CAR THOUGHT THEY SAW A DEER OR SOME OTHER ANIMAL AND NOTHING WAS REPORTED TO THE DNR ABOUT THE SIGHTING.

BIG CAT HAD BEEN TRAVELING FOR ALMOST A WEEK WITH VERY LITTLE FOOD. HE HAD ONLY EATEN SPARINGLY AFTER FINDING A FEW LEFT-OVERS AND CATCHING A RABBIT ALONG THE WAY, SO HUNGER WAS A DRIVING FORCE WHEN HE CAME UPON A HOBBY FARM, ONE NIGHT WITH A LONE HORSE IN A CORRAL.

GENERALLY, GOING AFTER A HORSE WAS NOT ON HIS MENU BUT HE WAS VERY HUNGER AND THE HORSE WAS VERY TEMPTING! BEING UP-WIND OF BIG

CAT, THE HORSE DIDN'T SEE HIM OR SMELL HIM AS IT CONTINUED TO GRAZE UNAWARE OF ANY DANGER.

BIG CAT NOTICED A TREE THAT HAD GROWN ON THE FENCE LINE AND OVERLAPPED THE CORRAL FENCE. LEAPING, HE CLIMBED INTO POSITION IN THE TREE AS QUIETLY AS POSSIBLE BUT THE HORSE HEARD SOMETHING AND LOOKED UP AS BIG CAT FROZE MOTIONLESSLY UNTIL THE HORSE WENT BACK TO GRAZING.

THEN THE WAITING GAME BEGAN! ALL BIG CAT COULD DO WAS WAIT AND HOPE THAT THE HORSE WOULD GRAZE CLOSE ENOUGH TO HIM SO THAT HE COULD LEAP ON IT. AN HOUR WENT BY AND THE HORSE MOVED CLOSER TO BIG CAT BUT NOT CLOSE ENOUGH FOR HIM TO LEAP. AS HE WAITED IN THE TREE, HE COULD HEAR THE CONSTANT RUMBLE OF THE CARS GOING DOWN THE DISTANT FREEWAY.

HE HAD BEEN WAITING MOST OF THE NIGHT AND DAWN WAS APPROACHING WHEN THE HORSE FINALLY; WAS WITHIN BIG CAT'S STRIKING RANGE. TENSING ALL HIS MUSCLES, BIG CAT LEAPED OUT OF THE TREE AT THE HORSE. THE HORSE HEARD A SOUND AND LUNGED AWAY FROM BIG CAT AS HE SAW THE LEAPING CAT.

WITH HIS FRONT PAWS EXTENDED AND CLAWS SHOWING, HE SAILED AT THE HORSE BUT WAS ONLY ABLE TO GET A PARTIAL HOLD ON THE MAIN OF THE HORSE AS IT SWUNG AWAY. WHINING IN FEAR; THE HORSE REARED BACKWARDS AS BIG CAT'S CLAWS SLASHED ACROSS THE TOP OF ITS NECK. AS THE HORSE REARED UP AND PULLED AWAY FROM HIM; BIG CAT LOST HIS GRIP ON THE HORSE. LANDING WITH HIS CAT-LIKE ABILITIES ON THE GROUND; HE HAD TO DODGE THE REAR HOOFS OF THE HORSE AS IT KICKED AT HIM AND RAN AWAY.

BIG CAT KNEW THAT CHASING AFTER THE HORSE WAS TOO DANGEROUS BECAUSE IF HE WERE TO GET INJURED IN THE STRUGGLE IT WOULD ENDANGER HIS LIFE. ANY INJURY WOULD LESSEN HIS ABILITY TO CATCH PREY AND WITHOUT THE ABILITY TO HUNT HE WOULD STARVE. SO, STAYING CLEAR OF THE HORSE, HE JUMPED THE CORRAL FENCE AND DISAPPEARED INTO THE FOREST.

CHAPTER 14

CHILDREN, A BADGER
AND A BARN

THE EARLY MORNING LIGHT WAS BREAKING THROUGH THE TREES AS BIG CAT LOPED AWAY FROM THE HORSE AND HE KNEW THAT HE HAD TO FIND SHELTER SOON. HEADING FOR THE NEAREST CLUMP OF TREES HE FOUND LITTLE SHELTER AS THE TREES WERE NOT VERY CLUSTERED AND OPEN FIELDS LAY ALL AROUND THEM. HE WAS TEMPTED TO HOLD UP THERE EXCEPT FOR THE GROUP OF HOUSES THAT WERE CLOSE TO THE TREES WHICH MADE HIM FEEL UNEASY.

AS BIG CAT WALKED THROUGH A NARROW STRIP OF WOODS NEAR SOME HOMES, HIS EYES CAUGHT MOVEMENT IN A WINDOW OF ONE OF THE HOUSES. HUNGER AND CURIOSITY DREW HIM OUT OF THE BRUSH AS HE STEPPED CLOSER TO THE HOUSE.

SLIPPING UP BESIDE THE HOUSE HE WALKED AROUND THE HOUSE UNTIL HE NOTICED A WINDOW IN A DOOR THAT CAME DOWN TO THE FLOOR LEVEL. GLANCING INTO THE HOUSE HE SAW A HUMAN INSIDE AND THE TWO STARED AT ONE ANOTHER FOR A MOMENT BEFORE BIG CAT LOST HIS NERVE AND RAN OUT TOWARDS THE WOODED AREA NEARBY.

STOPPING OUT ACROSS THE LAWN; HE WATCHED AS TWO CHILDREN PLAYED IN THE HOUSE BY A GLASS SLIDING-DOOR. BIG CAT FEARED MAN BUT HIS CURIOSITY MADE HIM SIT AND WATCH. AS HE WATCHED THE CHILDREN RUN AND PLAY IN THE HOUSE THROUGH THE WINDOW, HE WAS TORN BETWEEN GETTING CLOSER AND FLEEING TO SAFETY FROM HUMANS.

SUDDENLY, AN ADULT HUMAN APPEARED IN THE WINDOW LOOKING BACK AT HIM BUT SHE DIDN'T SHOW ANY AGGRESSION TOWARDS BIG CAT; SO HE CONTINUED TO WATCH THEM FOR ANOTHER TWENTY MINUTES. THE MOTHER AND HER CHILDREN WEREN'T AFRAID AS THEY WATCHED THE COUGAR THROUGH THE WINDOW AND EVEN GOT THEIR MOVIE CAMERA TO FILM THE CAT. FINALLY; BIG CAT TURNED AND SLUNK INTO THE WOODS AS PEOPLE WERE DRIVING UP TO THEIR HOMES NEARBY AND GETTING OUT.

THE TREE GROVE DIDN'T FEEL LIKE A GOOD SHELTER SO, BIG CAT CONTINUED ON QUICKLY CROSSING A FIELD HEADING FOR ANOTHER GROUP OF TREES. AS HE ENTERED THE SECOND CLUSTER OF TREES, HE SAW THAT THEY COVERED MORE ACREAGE AND HE SEARCHED FOR A SAFE PLACE TO REST FOR THE DAY.

BIG OAK TREES WITH LITTLE BRUSH UNDER THEM DIDN'T OFFER MUCH SHELTER AND GROWTHS OF ASPEN TREES WITH SCATTERED BIRCH AND BRUSHER WOODS WERE SOME OF THE AREAS BIG CAT CAME ACROSS AS HE KEPT WALKING. HE WAS VERY AWARE OF HIS HUNGER AND WAS STILL SEARCHING FOR SOMETHING TO EAT WHEN HE CAME UPON A BADGER DIGGING IN THE GROUND.

AS BIG CAT STARTED TO STALK THE BADGER IT LIFTED ITS HEAD AND SAW HIM COMING. BADGERS DON'T HAVE THE BEST EYE-SIGHT AND ARE USUALLY NOT IN A GOOD MOOD, SO THIS ENCOUNTER WAS QUESTIONABLE AS FOR THE TURNOUT? THEY BOTH STARED AT ONE ANOTHER FOR A FEW MOMENTS THEN THE BADGER SNARLED AND STEPPED TOWARDS BIG CAT.

BIG CAT WASN'T INTIMIDATED BY THIS AT ALL AND SIMPLY RAISED HIS RIGHT FRONT PAW AND BATTED AT THE BADGER. WELL, THE BADGER DIDN'T SEEM TO REALIZE THAT HE WAS UP AGAINST A BIG PREDATOR AND THAT HE SHOULD BE AFRAID. AGAIN HE SNARLED AND JUMPED AT BIG CAT. THIS CAUGHT BIG CAT OFF-GUARD AND HE SNARLED BACK AT THE BADGER AS HE STEPPED BACKWARDS AND LIFTED HIS PAW READY TO STRIKE. THIS CONTINUED BACK AND FORTH WITH THE BOLD, BADGER JUMPING AT BIG CAT AND BIG CAT STEPPING BACK AS HE SNARLED AND STRUCK AT THE BADGER.

BIG CAT BEGAN TO SENSE THAT THIS CREATURE WASN'T GOING TO BE AN EASY MEAL AND EVENTUALLY, HE JUST TURNED AND BEGAN TO WALK AWAY. HOWEVER, MR. BADGER REALIZED HE HAD THE UPPER HAND AND PURSUED THE CAT. BIG CAT TURNED, SNARLED AND STRUCK AT THE BADGER BUT THE BADGER WOULDN'T BACK-OFF.

WHEN BIG CAT TRIED TO WALK AWAY AGAIN THE SAME THING HAPPENED. BIG CAT WAS GETTING UPSET WITH THE BADGER BUT HE DIDN'T FEEL CONFIDENT ENOUGH TO ATTACK HIM. FINALLY, THE BADGER FELT HE HAD DRIVEN BIG CAT FAR ENOUGH AWAY FROM HIS DEN AND HE STOPPED PURSUING BIG CAT AND GRUMBLING UNDER HIS BREATH THE BADGER WALKED AWAY.

BIG CAT WASN'T IN A GOOD MOOD AFTER THAT ENCOUNTER WITH THE BADGER AS IT HAD ONLY IRRITATED HIM AS HIS HUNGER GREW. TRAVELING ON THROUGH THE WOODS HE DIDN'T FIND ANYTHING EDIBLE AND HE WAS GETTING TO THE POINT OF ALMOST EATING ANYTHING! AFTER WALKING FOR A FEW MILES HE CAME THROUGH SOME THICK BUSH OUT UNTO AN OLD FARM HOMESTEAD. THE OLD HOUSE MUST HAVE BURNT DOWN AS ONLY THE FOUNDATION REMAINED BUT THE BARN WAS STILL STANDING ALTHOUGH IT HAD LOST A LOT OF ITS SIDING AND HAD BIG HOLES IN IT. BIG CAT WAS VERY CAUTIOUS AS HE CHECKED FOR HUMANS BUT HIS NOSE TOLD HIM THERE HADN'T BEEN ANY AROUND FOR SOME TIME.

SLOWLY HE APPROACHED THE HOMESTEAD SNIFFING AROUND WHEN SUDDENLY, OUT OF THE CORNER OF HIS EYE HE SAW A GROUNDHOG SQUIRMING INTO A HOLE IN THE BARN. BIG CAT WASN'T GOING TO LET THIS CHANCE FOR FOOD PASS HIM BY AND HE BOUNDED OVER TO THE BARN TO INVESTIGATE. HE COULD SEE THAT THAT THE GROUND-HOG HAD DUG A HOLE INSIDE THE BARN IN THE OLD FLOOR BOARDS. DIRT WAS PILED UP AROUND THE HOLE AND COVERED SOME OF THE WOOD FLOORING.

AFTER LOOKING AROUND THE INTERIOR OF THE BARN AND NOT SCENTING ANY DANGER, BIG CAT STEPPED INSIDE AND WALKED UP TO THE HOLE. SNIFFING FOR THE GROUNDHOG HE STARTED TO DIG AT THE ENTRANCE OF THE DEN AND WAS ABLE TO CATCH THE GROUNDHOG.

AFTER A MEAL OF GROUNDHOG, BIG CATS HUNGER WAS SOMEWHAT SATISFIED AND HE WENT ABOUT INVESTIGATING THE BARN. THERE WASN'T MUCH LEFT OF THE STRUCTURE BUT HALF A HAYMOW AND A COUPLE OPEN CALF PENS WITH STALLS IN THE CENTER FLOOR AREA MOSTLY COVERED WITH OLD HAY. BIG CAT CHECKED OUT EVERY *NOOK AND CRANNY*, SNIFFING AND LOOKING IN EVERY PLACE HE COULD. HE SMELT MICE, RATS, SQUIRRELS AND GROUNDHOG ALL OVER THE BARN, AND THEN HE SPOTTED THE HAYMOW ABOVE HIM.

FINDING A PARTIAL STEP ON SOME OLD BOARDS, BIG CAT STEPPED UP TRYING TO SEE WHAT WAS ABOVE HIM IN THE HAYMOW. DETERMINED TO CLIMB INTO THE HAYMOW; BIG CAT FOUND ANOTHER HORIZONTAL BOARD AND LEAPED UP INTO THE HAYMOW LANDING IN THE OLD HAY. A FEW OLD BALES OF HAY WERE STACKED NEAR ONE CORNER BUT THE REST OF THE FLOOR WAS COVERED WITH DECAYING HAY THAT WAS WELL TRAMPLED ON AND COVERED IN SOME AREAS WITH PIGEON DROPPINGS. BARNS ARE A FAVORITE PLACE OF PIGEONS AND ABANDONED BARNS ARE A PARADISE FOR THEM AS THEY FLY IN AND OUT OF THE OPEN DOORS NEAR THE ROOF AND NEST IN THE HIGH RAFTERS SAFELY FROM PREDATORS.

BIG CAT CAREFULLY CHECKED OUT EVERY CORNER AND CRANNY IN THE BARN LOOKING FOR ANY OTHER VARMINTS. HE COULD HEAR MICE SCURRY IN THE HAY NEAR HIS FEET AND THE SCENT OF HOUSE CATS AND RACCOONS FILLED HIS NOSE. WITH FURTHER INSPECTION OF THE BARN, BIG CAT FOUND A HOLE IN THE SIDE OF THE BARN TO BE USED FOR A QUICK EXIT IF HE NEEDED IT. FEELING MORE SECURITY HE JUMPED UP ON THE BALES AND AFTER TURNING AROUND A COUPLE TIMES TO FIND A GOOD SPOT, HE LAY DOWN TO REST.

AT DUSK, A NOISE FROM THE BARN FLOOR WOKE BIG CAT. JUMPING UP IN ALARM, BIG CAT HOPPED OFF THE BALES AND QUICKLY MOVED OVER TO THE EDGE OF THE HAYMOW AND CHECKED DOWN BELOW WHERE THE SOUND CAME FROM. FOUR RACCOONS HAD ENTERED THE BARN SEARCHING FOR FOOD. IN ONE GIANT LEAP, BIG CAT LANDED ON THE BARN FLOOR AND IN TWO BOUNDS HE SEIZED A RACCOON TRYING TO SQUEEZE THROUGH A LITTLE HOLE IN THE WALL OF THE BARN AND HE HAD HIMSELF ANOTHER MEAL.

AFTER EATING; BIG CAT'S CURIOSITY INSPIRED HIM TO GO EXPLORING THE AREA OUTSIDE THE BARN. SLIPPING OUT INTO THE FRESH AIR; BIG CAT BEGAN BY CHECKING OUT THE OTHER BUILDINGS. THE OLD SHED ONLY HAD THE FOUNDATION LEFT AND A FEW BOARDS WITH GROUND SQUIRRELS AND MICE LIVING UNDER THEM. BIG CAT LEFT HIS SCENT THERE AND WALKED OVER TO THE HOUSE FOUNDATION WHERE HE SAW A HOUSE CAT RACE OUT FROM UNDER THE SOME OLD BOARDS. HIS NOSE TOLD HIM THAT MICE AND OTHER RODENTS WERE PRESENT SO HE MARKED IT FOR FUTURE REFERENCE.

THIS WAS THE BEGINNING OF EXTENDED STAY IN THE BARN FOR BIG CAT. HE HAD LOTS OF VARMINTS TO EAT AND HE DIDN'T HAVE TO LOOK FAR TO

GET THEM. HE WOULD LAY IN WAIT AND SOONER OR LATER A GROUNDHOG, A RABBIT OR A RACCOON AND EVEN A HOUSE CAT WOULD MAKE THE MISTAKE OF COMING TO CLOSE AND THEY WOULD BE TAKEN AND EATEN.

YES, HOUSE CATS ARE NOT SAFE WHEN THEY MEET WILD ANIMALS IN THE WOODS, SUCH AS BOBCATS, FOXES, COYOTES AND OF COURSE MOUNTAIN LIONS! MANY HOUSE CATS ENTER THE WILD AND NEVER RETURN BECAUSE THEY MEET SUCH AN END. IT HAS EVEN BEEN REPORTED THAT IN THE SUBURBS OF A MICHIGAN CITY A COUGAR WAS SEEN IN SOMEONE'S BACKYARD WHERE THEY FEED STRAY CATS AND THE CATS DISAPPEARED ONE BY ONE. THESE EASY MEALS WERE A BLESSING FOR BIG CAT AND HE HAD LOTS OF TIME TO EXPLORE THE AREA.

SOMETIMES BIG CAT WANDERED OUT OF THE WOODS NEAR HOUSES IN THE DAYLIGHT WATCHING PEOPLE AND PETS FROM A DISTANCE. ENCOUNTERS WITH HUMANS WAS RARE AND UNWELCOME IN DAKOTA COUNTRY WHERE BIG CAT WAS BORN BUT AFTER HAVING LOTS OF "CLOSE CALLS" WITH PEOPLE IN OTHER PARTS OF THE COUNTRY, HE HAD BECOME MORE AT EASE AROUND THEM.

AT TIMES HE WOULD COME UPON A HUMAN WALKING DOWN A PATH AND HE WOULD JUST STEP OUT OF SIGHT AND WATCH THEM PASS BY. ONE TIME WHILE OUT LOOKING FOR FOOD, BIG CAT WAS SEEN BY A BLACK LAB THAT CAME RUNNING OUT AFTER HIM INTO A GROUP OF PINE TREES. BIG CAT LOPPED AWAY FROM THE DOG AND IT SOON LOST ITS NERVE TO CONTINUE THE CHASE.

OTHER TIMES, HE WOULD COME UPON PEOPLE STEPPING OUTSIDE OF THEIR HOME IN THE EVENING FOR A SMOKE AND HE NOTICED THE DIFFERENT ODORS OF THE CIGARETTE AS HE WATCHED THEM. ONE EVENING, HE WAS TRAVELING DOWN A DARK STREET IN THE SUBURBS WHEN A WOMAN SCREAMED AND RAN AWAY FROM HIM AFTER SEEING HIM IN THE SHADOWS. SHE KEPT GLANCING BACK AT BIG CAT AS SHE RAN BUT HE JUST STOPPED AND WATCHED HER RUN UP TO HER HOUSE AND GO IN, THEN HE LEFT THE AREA.

BECAUSE FOOD WAS SO AVAILABLE; BIG CAT'S LIFE SETTLED INTO A ROUTINE OF CATCHING PREY AND SLEEPING IN THE BARN UNTIL ONE DAY A FEW WEEKS LATER, A STRANGER SURPRISED HIM.

ONE MORNING JUST AFTER SETTLING INTO THE BARN TO REST IN THE HAYMOW, BIG CAT HEARD A LOUD STOMPING SOUND AND WHEN HE LOOKED DOWN HE WAS SURPRISED TO SEE A MAN'S FACE LOOKING BACK AT HIM! IT

APPEARS THE OWNER WAS CHECKING HIS PROPERTY AND WAS SHOCKED TO FIND A COUGAR IN HIS BARN!

BIG CAT WAS JUST AS SURPRISED AND LEAPED OUT THE ESCAPE HOLE IN THE BARN WALL AND HE DIDN'T STOP UNTIL HE WAS DEEP IN THE WOODS. BIG CAT KNEW THAT THE BARN WOULDN'T BE SAFE ANYMORE BECAUSE WHENEVER HUMANS DISCOVERED HIS HIDING PLACES IN THE PAST IT MEANT TROUBLE SO, HE CONTINUED ON HIS WAY.

CHAPTER 15

FALLING IN LOVE

THE LEAVES WERE TURNING DIFFERENT

COLORS AND FALLING TO THE GROUND AS BIG CAT CONTINUED HIS TREK ACROSS THE COUNTRY. HE HAD TRAVELED FOR MANY MILES THROUGH GROUPS OF TREES AND OPEN FIELDS HIDING IN RAVINES, TALL GRASS, CORN FIELDS OR ANY COVERAGE HE COULD FIND. HE WAS STILL INCLINED TO TRAVEL IN AN EASTERLY DIRECTION FOR AN UNKNOWN REASON; HOWEVER HIS TRAVELING WAS SOMETIMES ERRATIC BECAUSE OF TERRAIN OR HUMAN INTERFERENCE. CROSSING HIGHWAYS IS ALWAYS A CHALLENGE FOR ANIMALS AND FOR BIG CAT, IT WASN'T ANY DIFFERENT.

MANY TIMES HE HAD TO WAIT FOR TRAFFIC TO LET UP BEFORE CROSSING AND ONCE HE WAS ACTUALLY, CAUGHT IN THE MIDDLE LANE WAITING FOR THE CARS TO CLEAR BEFORE CROSSING IN DAYLIGHT! HE TRIED NOT TO CROSS IN THE DAYLIGHT BUT SOMETIMES HE WAS FORCED TO CROSS AT THAT TIME BECAUSE OF THE NEARNESS OF PEOPLE OR DOGS.

ONE EVENING WHILE HE WAS SEARCHING FOR A MEAL AND WAS PASSING THROUGH A NEW PINE GROVE, HE PICKED UP A SCENT THAT HE *HAD NEVER ENCOUNTERED BEFORE* THAT AROUSED SOMETHING IN HIM. THE ODOR WAS SOMETHING THAT STIRRED FEELINGS INSIDE OF HIM THAT WERE ALL NEW TO HIM! YEARNINGS THAT SEEMED TO MAKE HIM FORGET ALL ABOUT HIS HUNGER AND A STRONG DESIRE DROVE HIM TO SEEK OUT THE SOURCE OF THE SMELL.

QUICKLY FOLLOWING THE SCENT TRAIL, BIG CAT FORGED FORWARD, ALMOST RECKLESSLY, SEARCHING TO FIND THE ANSWER TO THIS NEW SCENT THAT CREATED

AN URGENT NEED IN HIM. AS HE FOLLOWED THE TRAIL HE HEARD A SOFT COOING SOUND FROM A DISTANCE. THIS WAS A SOUND THAT HE HADN'T HEARD BEFORE AND HE WASN'T SURE *WHAT IT MEANT—OR WHAT IT WAS COMING FROM?*

AFTER FOLLOWING THE TRAIL ACROSS A CREEK, OVER A RIVER BANK, THROUGH THICK BRUSH AND AROUND NUMEROUS TREES, BIG CAT CAME FACE TO FACE WITH ANOTHER MOUNTAIN LION! HE DIDN'T FEEL ALARMED OR READY TO DEFEND HIMSELF BECAUSE HE SENSED SOMETHING VERY DIFFERENT ABOUT THIS COUGAR.

HE COULD TELL THAT THE OTHER LION WAS A FEMALE AND SHE WASN'T AGGRESSIVE AND THE FACT THAT SHE ROLLED ON THE GROUND IN FRONT OF HIM PROVED IT! BIG CAT HAD JUST REACHED TWO YEARS OLD AND THIS ENCOUNTER WAS SOMETHING NEW FOR HIM.

THE TWO STOOD GAZING AT ONE ANOTHER FOR A MOMENT BEFORE THE FEMALE SLUNK UP TO HIM AND THEY TOUCHED NOSES. EXCITEMENT STIRRED IN BIG CAT AND HE FELT PLAYFUL, YET DOMINANT OVER THE FEMALE CAT. AFTER WATCHING THE FEMALE MOUNTAIN LION FOR SOMETIME AS SHE ROLLED ON THE GROUND; BIG CAT STEPPED OVER HER AND GENTLY, YET FIRMLY, GRABBED THE BACK OF HER NECK AND THEY MATED.

THIS COUPLING WAS NOT ROMANTIC AS IT IS OFTEN WRITTEN ABOUT BY HUMANS BUT AGGRESSIVE WITH SNARLS AND BITES BEING GIVEN AND RECEIVED AT THE SAME TIME. AT TIMES, THE MATING OF THE TWO HAD DRAWN THE ATTENTION OF HUMANS AND THEY HAD TO RUN OFF TO ANOTHER LOCATION. HOWEVER, THEY STAYED TOGETHER FOR OVER A WEEK, MATING, SLEEPING AND SOMETIMES CHASING EACH OTHER THROUGH THE GRASS. ONE MORNING WHEN THE TWO WERE HUNTING FOR FOOD THEY SPOTTED TWO SWANS SWIMMING IN A POND.

WADING OUT INTO THE WATER THE CATS HOPED TO GET CLOSE ENOUGH TO CAPTURE THE BIRDS WHEN ON THE OTHER SIDE OF THE POND TWO PEOPLE APPEARED AND SPOILED THE HUNT. THE COUGARS BOUNDED OFF INTO THE WOODS.

AFTER ABOUT A WEEK AND A HALF OF BEING TOGETHER THE FEMALE GREW LESS FRIENDLY AND BIG CAT HAD THE FEELING HE SHOULD MOVE ON. STALLING ONLY SEEMED TO BEING OUT MORE AGGRESSION AND LESS ATTENTION FROM HER, SO BIG CAT JUST TURNED AND WENT HIS WAY.

As Big Cat walked away he began to realize how hunger he was! During the mating they had only, eaten occasionally and now he needed to fill his stomach. Directing all his attention to finding food; Big Cat began hunting in earnest for any scent of food that he could find.

Leaving the area where he and the other cougar had been; Big Cat crossed a field and entered a pine plantation. The scent of rabbits crossed his nose and he began hunting them. The tracks crossed back and forth as Big Cat continued through tall grass and brush looking for rabbits. Suddenly, he caught movement out of the corner of his eye and quickly turning, he chased after a jack rabbit.

Bounding through the tall grass, dodging brush and leaping over fallen trees; Big Cat was a sight to see as his agility and movements were beautiful to watch! Leaves flew in the air as Big Cat closed the gap between himself and the rabbit. When the rabbit pace slowed down a little; Big Cat was able to grab the rabbit and they both came to a sliding halt.

The rabbit was like an appetizer for Big Cat and he needed more. Though he continued to search the area; Big cat wasn't able to find anymore rabbits or any other meal that day. Traveling on; Big Cat crossed more fields and through small clusters of trees until he came upon a creek where he lapped some water. After crossing the creek and climbing up the other bank; Big Cat caught the scent of deer.

Crouching low and following the trail, Big Cat saw movement ahead as a deer flashed its white tail in the air and ran off. A couple people on the other side of the river noticed a cougar enter the woods, then saw two deer come out of the woods and run into the river to get away from him. Big cat could only watch as the deer waded down the river and ran into the woods as the people looked on. A cougar's chances of capturing a meal is not good, only like one or two captures per ten tries!

CHAPTER 16

TRAVELING MILES

FALL HAD TURNED THE LEAVES INTO BEAUTIFUL COLORS AND THEY WERE FALLING TO THE GROUND WHEN BIG CAT REACHED LAKE MICHIGAN AFTER CROSSING THE STATE OF WISCONSIN. HE CHOSE TO HEAD IN A NORTHERLY DIRECTION BECAUSE THERE SEEMED TO BE FEWER HOUSES AND MORE FORESTS AFTER SEEING THE LARGE CLUSTER OF HUMANS AND BUILDINGS TO THE SOUTH.

STILL FINDING WOODED AREAS FOR SHELTER WAS DIFFICULT FOR HIM AS HIGHWAYS AND HOUSING WERE EVERYWHERE. TROTTING AT TIMES, THEN WALKING AND CROUCHING LOW HE'D PASSED THROUGH SNOWY DITCHES AFTER THE WINTER'S FIRST SNOW THEN ENTER CLUMPS OF TREES AND BRUSH STAYING OUT OF SIGHT OF PEOPLE.

HOWEVER, STAYING OUT OF SIGHT WAS UNLIKELY WHEN BIG CAT TRAVELED IN DAYLIGHT. COMING UPON A HIGHLY WOODED, NATURAL WET LAND, POPULATED WITH GEESE AND DEER, BIG CAT BEGAN TO HUNT FOR A MEAL ONE AFTERNOON WHEN TWO MEN CAME WALKING DOWN A SIDEWALK BY THE GENERAL MOTORS CORP. AND SAW HIM IN A WOODED AREA BEHIND THE MAJOR INDUSTRIAL AREA.

BIG CAT DIDN'T EVEN NOTICE THE MEN AS HE CLOSED IN ON SOME DOMESTICATED GEESE WALKING NEAR A SMALL POND. YEARS OF LIVING NEAR PEOPLE HAD DULLED THE GEESE' NATURAL SURVIVAL INSTINCTS AND BIG CAT WAS ABLE TO SNEAK UP ON THEM. HE HAD SEEN THEM AT A DISTANCE AND

AFTER CRAWLING ON HIS BELLY, STAYING BEHIND BRUSH AND TALL GRASS HE WAS FINALLY WITHIN STRIKING RANGE OF THE GEESE.

THE GEESE WERE OCCASIONALLY, HONKING, "TALKING WITH EACH OTHER" AS BIG CAT WATCHED THEM WADDLE ALONG. PICKING THE CLOSEST GOOSE TO HIM; BIG CAT MADE HIS RUSH AT IT. AS HE SPRANG INTO THE OPEN ALL THE GEESE BEGAN SQUAWKING, JUMPING AND FLYING IN ALL DIRECTIONS WHEN THEY SAW A COUGAR CHARGING AT THEM. BIG CAT CLOSED IN ON HIS CHOSEN GOOSE JUST AS IT WAS FLAPPING ITS WINGS ABOUT TO TAKE FLIGHT AND HE PULLED IT DOWN. GRABBING THE GOOSE IN HIS MOUTH, BIG CAT TROTTED OFF INTO THE TALL GRASS. AFTER HIS MEAL HE SETTLED DOWN IN A SECLUDED, BRUSHY AREA WHERE HE COULD REST FOR THE NIGHT. BIG CAT STAYED IN THE AREA HUNTING AND RESTING FOR A FEW DAYS.

TRAVELING FURTHER NORTH; BIG CAT CROSSED INTO IRON, MICHIGAN COUNTRY WHERE HE CAME UPON A GOLF COURSE AND RV PARK ADJACENT TO A RIVER. WHILE HUNTING RABBITS NEAR THE GOLF COURSE ONE NIGHT; BIG CAT NOTICED A MAN WALKING DOWN A TRAIL ON THE BANK OF THE RIVER BY HIM. BIG CAT LOPED ACROSS THE OPEN FIELD AND DODGED INTO THE TALL GRASS ON THE RIVER BANK AND CROUCHED LOW.

THE MAN MADE THE DECISION TO ACT BRAVE INSTEAD OF USING COMMON SENSE AND CAME TOWARDS BIG CAT SHAKING THE GRASS. WHEN HE WAS DIRECTLY ABOVE BIG CAT, HE LOOKED DOWN AND THE TWO LOOKED EACH OTHER IN THE EYE.

TURNING AND LEAPING, BIG CAT RAN TOWARDS THE RIVER INTO THICKER BRUSH AND HID. THE MAN WAS AS STARTLED AS BIG CAT, AND QUICKLY WALKED AWAY LOOKING BACK OFTEN. BIG CAT JUST WAITED UNTIL HE FELT SAFE THEN CONTINUED HUNTING.

CROSSING BACK TO THE GOLF COURSE, BIG CAT FOUND THE TRAIL OF THE RABBIT AND STARTED TRACKING IT. THE TRAIL LED TO A SMALL SHED WHERE THE RABBIT HAD CRAWLED INTO A HOLE UNDER IT. BIG CAT SNIFFED AT THE HOLE AND THE RABBIT RAN OUT THE OTHER SIDE. SEEING THE RABBIT OUT OF THE CORNER OF HIS EYE, BIG CAT RACED AFTER IT.

TEARING ACROSS THE GOLF COURSE IN THE DARK; BIG CAT DIDN'T GET CLOSE ENOUGH TO THE RABBIT BEFORE IT FOUND A HOLLOW LOG AND DOVE INTO IT. BIG CAT STUCK HIS PAW IN AFTER THE RABBIT BUT HE COULDN'T REACH IT SO

HE CHECKED FOR OTHER HOLES IN THE LOG. FINDING A HOLE ON THE OTHER SIDE OF THE LOG; BIG CAT PRODDED HIS PAW AROUND INSIDE HOPING TO REACH THE RABBIT. THE RABBIT FELT BIG CAT'S DIGGING AND TRIED TO RACE BACK OUT THE END OF THE LOG. HOWEVER, BIG CAT WAS READY AND SCOOPED HIM UP AS SOON AS HE LEFT THE LOG.

ANOTHER NIGHT WHILE SEARCHING FOR FOOD; BIG CAT WAS CROSSING A ROADWAY WHEN HE CAUGHT SCENT OF A FRESH KILL. FOLLOWING HIS NOSE, HE WALKED UP-WIND UNTIL HE SAW A DEAD DOE LYING IN THE CENTER OF ROAD. IT WAS A LATE AT NIGHT AND BIG CAT WAS HUNGRY, SO HE SETTLED DOWN AND STARTED TO EAT. HE HAD BEEN FEASTING FOR ABOUT A HALF-HOUR WHEN HE SAW LIGHTS APPROACHING.

UP UNTIL THAT TIME THE ROAD HAD BEEN FREE OF ANY INTERFERENCE AND BIG CAT RESENTED THE INTERRUPTION OF HIS MEAL. THE LIGHTS CONTINUED TO GET BRIGHTER AND BIG CAT CROUCHED LOW BY HIS DEER AND HOPED HE WOULDN'T BE SEEN. HE COULD HEAR THE ENGINE AS THE CAR DREW NEARER TO HIM WITH ITS BRIGHT LIGHTS BUT HE WAS HUNGRY AND WENT BACK TO HIS MEAL UNTIL A BLAST FROM THE CAR HORN STARTLED HIM.

LEAPING STRAIGHT AWAY; BIG CAT LANDED ON THE EDGE OF THE ROAD IN A RUN AND RACED OFF. THE CAR LEFT IN A FEW MINUTES AND BIG CAT WAITED A FEW MORE MINUTES TO MAKE SURE ALL WAS SAFE BEFORE HE WALKED BACK TO THE DEER AND BEGAN TO FEED.

HE ATE FOR ABOUT AN HOUR BEFORE ANOTHER CAR BEGAN TO APPROACH. BIG CAT DIDN'T WAIT FOR THE CAR TO GET TOO CLOSE THIS TIME BEFORE HE RAN INTO THE WOODS AND WATCHED THE CAR CRUISE BY WITHOUT STOPPING. HE WASN'T ABLE TO EAT FOR VERY LONG AFTER THAT BEFORE HE HAD TO RUN FOR SHELTER AGAIN AS CAR AFTER CAR STARTED TO COME DOWN THE ROAD. IT WAS THE MORNING RUSH HOUR.

DAYS TURNED INTO MONTHS AS BIG CAT MOVED FROM AREA TO AREA IN SEARCH OF FOOD AND SHELTER. THE NIGHTS HAD BEGUN TO GET COLDER WHICH DIDN'T BOTHER HIM BECAUSE HIS FUR COAT HAD FILLED OUT INTO A THICK, LUSTER OF BROWN HAIR WITH TOUCHES OF BLACK ON HIS FACE AND A WHITE CHEST AND UNDER-BELLY.

AFTER A NIGHT OF HUNTING WITH LITTLE SUCCESS, BIG CAT WAS THIRSTY. HE HAD CAUGHT A RABBIT AFTER A LONG PURSUIT AND WAS IN NEED OF

WATER. A BIG LAKE WAS JUST ACROSS THE ROAD FROM THE WOODS THAT HE HAD BEEN HUNTING IN.

AS HE CROSSED OVER THE ROAD A CAR CAME TOWARDS HIM BUT THE DISTANCE WAS FAR ENOUGH AWAY THAT BIG CAT DIDN'T FEEL HE NEEDED TO HURRY; BESIDES HE WAS TIRED FROM A LONG NIGHT OF HUNTING. THE DRIVER OF THE CAR WAS A RESIDENT OF THE AREA AND HAD SEEN BIG CAT CROSS ONCE BEFORE WHILE HE DROVE BY.

BIG CAT CROSSED OVER THE ROAD AFTER THE CAR DISAPPEARED ONTO A SANDY BEACH LEAVING HIS PRINTS AS HE WALKED ALONG SNIFFING THE OCCASIONAL DEAD CRUSTACEANS, LIKE SNAILS AND CLAMS. AFTER SATISFYING HIS THIRST BY LAPPING AT THE WATER HE PASSED BACK OVER THE ROAD WITHOUT ANY INTERFERENCE FROM HUMANS OR CARS.

ANOTHER EVENING WHILE HE WAS EXPLORING AND LOOKING FOR A MEAL, HE WALKED AROUND A SCHOOL BUILDING INTO THE BALL FIELD WHICH WAS FILLED WITH THE SCENT OF HUMANS. SUDDENLY, HE WAS LIT-UP BY CAR LIGHTS ACROSS THE BALL FIELD AND HE STARTED SEARCHING FOR A PLACE TO HIDE.

A FATHER AND DAUGHTER HAD JUST COME OUT OF THE SCHOOL BUILDING AND WERE LEAVING WHEN THEIR LIGHTS CAUGHT BIG CAT IN THEIR BEAMS. THE DAUGHTER SAW THE COUGAR FIRST AND THE FATHER TRIED TO FOLLOW THE CAT WITH THE CAR LIGHTS BUT HAD TO GET OUT OF THE CAR SEVERAL TIMES TO GET A BETTER VIEW BIG CAT. HE WOULD GET BACK INTO THE CAR AND DRIVE AROUND FENCES AND BUILDINGS AS THEY WATCHED BIG CAT RUN UNDER THE CONCESSION STAND THEN OVER TO THE EQUESTRIAN ARENAS. AFTER THAT BIG CAT FOUND SOME RAVINES CLUSTERED WITH BRUSH AND SOME TREES AND GOT AWAY FROM THE HEAVILY POPULATED AREAS.

CHAPTER 17

HUMANS IN THE WOODS

SEPTEMBER THEN NOVEMBER ARRIVED AND WITH IT CAME THE SNOW AND THE HUMAN HUNTERS INTRUDING INTO BIG CATS DOMAIN. IT SEEMED BIG CAT COULDN'T EVEN HUNT WITHOUT SEEING SOME HUMAN WALKING THROUGH THE WOODS OR INTERRUPTING HIS HUNT. ONE NIGHT HE HAD ENTERED A SWAMPY AREA WITH A ROAD RUNNING THROUGH THE SWAMP.

AS HE WALKED DOWN THE ROAD CHECKING FOR ANY SCENT OF FOOD, BIG CAT WAS SURPRISED BY A CAR WITH BRIGHT LIGHTS TURNING HIS WAY. THE CAR WAS IN THE OTHER LANE AND HE WASN'T GOING TO BE BOTHERED BY IT, SO HE KEPT WALKING. HOWEVER, THE CAR KEPT APPROACHING CLOSER AND BIG CAT WAS BEGINNING TO BE CONCERNED.

FINALLY, THE CAR BRAKE–LIGHTS CAME ON AND BIG CAT TURNED TO THE SIDE AND STOOD STILL AS THE CAR CAME TO A STOP ABOUT FIFTEEN FEET AWAY! NOT SURE OF WHAT TO DO, BIG CAT GAZED AT THE LIGHTS FOR A MOMENT BEFORE LEAPING OVER THE DITCH AND LANDED IN THE MARSHY, SWAMP. THE DRIVER HAD A FULL VIEW OF THE COUGAR AND EVEN WENT BACK THE NEXT DAY TO CHECK FOR PRINTS TO NO AVAIL.

BIG CAT HAD JUST WAITED FOR THE CAR TO DISAPPEAR AND CONTINUED INTO THE SWAMP. HIS FEET SUNK INTO THE MOSS UNDER HIS FEET AS HE WALKED THROUGH TAMARACKS CHECKING FOR THE SCENT OF RABBITS AND OTHER OCCUPANTS OF THE SWAMP. THERE WERE NO FRESH TRAILS SO HE MADE HIS WAY THROUGH THE SWAMP AND UP THE OTHER SIDE.

COMING OUT OF THE SWAMP AND UNTO A GOLF COURSE, BIG CAT FELT VERY EXPOSED TO THE HUMAN EYE BUT IT WAS NEAR MIDNIGHT AND NO ONE WAS AROUND. WALKING ACROSS THE SHORT, WELL-KEPT GRASS, BIG CAT HAD A CLEAR VIEW OF THE COURSE WHEN, SUDDENLY ON THE OTHER SIDE OF THE COURSE HE SAW MOVEMENT.

STOPPING AND FOCUSING ON THE TARGET, BIG CAT LOWERED HIMSELF INTO A CROUCHING POSITION AND SLOWLY, STARTED STALKING THE ANIMAL. HIS EYES WERE CENTERED ON THE SMALL CREATURE ACROSS THE GRASS AS HE GRACEFULLY MOVED FORWARD STOPPING WHEN THE OTHER ANIMAL STOPPED MOVING. WHEN BIG CAT WAS ABOUT A HUNDRED YARDS AWAY FROM THE ANIMAL HE COULD SEE THAT IT WAS A HOUSE CAT. THE CAT HADN'T SEEN BIG CAT, YET AND WAS SEARCHING AROUND IN THE LEAVES ON THE EDGE OF THE GOLF COURSE IN THE BRUSH LOOKING FOR MICE. BIG CAT CONTINUED HIS STALKING WITH SMALL, SHORT STEPS MOVING WHEN THE CAT MOVED THEN WAITING WHEN THE CAT WAS STILL.

BIG CAT WAS WITHIN FIFTY FEET OF THE HOUSE CAT WHEN IT FIRST SAW HIM! THE TWO STARED AT ONE ANOTHER FOR A FEW SECONDS, THEN THE HOUSE CAT TURNED AND RAN FOR HIS LIFE THROUGH THE BRUSH TOWARDS HIS MASTERS HOUSE ABOUT FIFTY YARDS AWAY. BIG CAT TORE AFTER HIM CHARGING THROUGH THE BRUSH IN PURSUIT OF THE HOUSE CAT.

NOTHING WAS GOING TO SLOW DOWN THE HOUSE CAT AS HE KNEW HIS LIFE WAS AT STAKE! HE HAD JUST REACHED THE HOUSE STEPS AS BIG CAT ENTERED THE YARD. INSTANTLY, LOUD BARKING FILLED BIG CAT EARS AS THE FAMILY DOG CAME OUT OF HIS DOG HOUSE AND RAN AT BIG CAT. QUICKLY SPINNING, BIG CAT RAN BACK THE WAY HE HAD COME. FORTUNATELY FOR HIM, THE DOG WAS CHAINED AND HE WAS HALTED AT THE END OF HIS CHAIN.

AFTER THAT, BIG CAT TRAVELED MILES AWAY FROM THE AREA AND FINDING A MORE WOODED AREA HE CAUGHT A RABBIT. EARLY ONE MORNING BEFORE DAWN; HE WAS STALKING A DEER WHEN A HUMAN CAME INTO HIS HUNTING RANGE. AT FIRST, BIG CAT SAT AND LISTENED TO THE STEADY STOMPING OF WHAT SOUNDED LIKE A TWO-LEGGED CREATURE, POSSIBLY A HUMAN WALKING TOWARDS HIM.

IT WAS STILL DARK AND UNKNOWINGLY THE HUMAN WALKED BY BIG CAT ONLY TWENTY FEET AWAY! BECAUSE THE HUMAN CONTINUED WALKING AS IF

HE HADN'T SEEN HIM, BIG CAT'S CURIOSITY GOT THE BETTER OF HIM AND HE STARTED FOLLOWING THE HUMAN SCENT WHICH TOLD HIM WAS A MAN.

SUDDENLY, THE MAN STOPPED AND SO DID BIG CAT. THEN AFTER A MOMENT OR TWO THE MAN WOULD CONTINUE WALKING AND SO BIG CAT FOLLOWED HIM. THEN AGAIN, THE MAN WOULD STOP WALKING AND SO WOULD BIG CAT.

THIS WENT ON FOR SOME TIME BEFORE BIG CAT WAS PUZZLED TO HEAR THE MAN STOP AND SUDDENLY MAKE A *GROWLING SOUND!* THEN HE HEARD THE LOUD CLUNKING SOUND OF METAL COMING FROM THE MAN AS HE INJECTED A BULLET INTO THE CHAMBER OF HIS RIFLE. BIG CAT WAS PUZZLED AND DECIDED TO LET THE MAN WALK OFF WITHOUT FOLLOWING HIM. THEN HE HEARD THE SOUND OF THE MAN CLIMBING A TREE AND AFTER THAT SILENCE.

AFTER WAITING FOR A WHILE HIS CURIOSITY GOT THE BEST OF HIM AND HE FOLLOWED THE MAN'S TRAIL UP TO THE TREE AND HEARD A STRANGE SNORING SOUND FROM UP IN THE TREE. THEN HIS INSTINCT TOLD HIM TO BEWARE AND BIG CAT DOUBLED-BACK ON THE TRAIL RECHECKING THE SCENT AND CONTINUED TO THOROUGHLY CHECK OUT THE AREA. BIG CAT HAD FOLLOWED A HUNTER A FEW DAYS BEFORE IN A SIMILAR MANNER AND WAS CAUGHT BETWEEN HIS HUNTING INSTINCTS AND FEAR OF MAN. LATER WHEN THE HUNTER RETURNED HOME HE LOGGED ONTO THE SITE (WWW.SAVETHECOUGAR.ORG). AND DOCUMENTED THE FOLLOWING . . .

QUOTE. "I WAS JUST WALKING OUT TO MY BLIND, SLOW AND QUIET AS ALWAYS FOR MY ANNUAL OPENING DAY DEER HUNT. I DON'T SPOOK EASILY BUT SOON AS I STARTED WALKING IN THE BUSH THERE WAS SOMETHING STALKING ME. I COULDN'T SEE IT BUT IT WAS LOUD AND CLOSE. I TOOK A FEW STEPS. IT TOOK A FEW STEPS. THIS WENT ON FOR ABOUT 200 FEET".

"THEN I WAS REALLY SCARED THINKING THAT MAYBE IT WAS A BEAR OR A WOLF. NEVER-EVER EXPECTING A COUGAR, FOR HEAVEN'S SAKES!! I STOPPED . . . MADE A LOUD GROWL (BOY HAVE I GOT TEASED FOR THAT), RACKED A BULLET INTO MY CHAMBER AND WAS READY TO FIRE A SHOT TO SCARE IT. I GOT THE REST OF THE WAY BACK TO MY BLIND WITHOUT ANY MORE STALKING. I WAS SO SCARED! MY HEART WAS POUNDING AND I WAS SO BUMMED THAT I HAD JUST RUINED MY OPENING DAY HUNT.

"I TOOK A NAP SINCE THERE WAS ANY WAY A DEER WOULD BE IN MY BLIND AFTER THAT RIDICULOUS GROWL AND THE FACT THAT I PROBABLY SOUNDED

LIKE A HERD OF ELEPHANTS ENTERING MY BLIND. I WOKE UP GROGGY, LOOKED OUT MY WINDOW AND SWORE I SAW A COUGAR. I IMMEDIATELY THOUGHT TO MYSELF, DID I JUST DREAM THAT? ARE THERE FRICKIN COUGARS UP HERE? IS THAT WHAT FRICKIN STALKED ME THIS MORNING?

(LATER)" THEN ONE OF THE BOYS SAID THAT THEY WERE STALKED WALKING OUT OF HIS BLIND FOR ABOUT A THOUSAND YARDS. HE HAD A PISTOL AND WASN'T SCARED AND ALSO COULD NOT SEE IT. HE SAID IT WAS STALKING ABOUT TWENTY FEET AWAY IN EXACTLY THE SAME MANNER. HE TOOK A FEW STEPS . . . THE CAT TOOK A FEW. HE STOPPED . . . THE CAT STOPPED. MY HEART IS STILL POUNDING!!" (NOV.15, 2010-SAVE THE COUGAR DOT ORG).

SOMETIME LATER, BIG CAT WAS FOLLOWING DEER SCENT THROUGH A CEDAR GROVE AND AS HE CAME TO THE EDGE OF A SWAMP HE *FROZE IN HIS TRACKS!* BIG CAT HAD CREPT UP ON A YEARLING DEER AND LIKE ALL CATS HE STOOD PERFECTLY STILL STANDING WITH ONE HIDE LEG SUSPENDED IN THE AIR.

HOWEVER, HE WAS UNAWARE THAT A HUNTER WAS IN A DEER STAND EIGHTY YARDS AWAY FROM HIM. THINKING BIG CAT WAS A DEER THE HUNTER LIFTED HIS RIFLE AND TO HIS SURPRISE SAW A COUGAR. RE-ADJUSTING HIS SCOPE TO A HIGHER POWER HE COULD MAKE OUT THE LONG TAIL OF THE COUGAR BUT BEFORE HE HAD TIME TO THINK THE COUGAR WAS GONE.

BIG CAT CONTINUED TO STALK THE DEER, SOFTLY PLACING HIS FEET ON THE GROUND ONE AT A TIME. THE YEARLING WAS LAGGING BEHIND ITS MOTHER AND UNKNOWINGLY WAS *A MEAL* ON BIG CATS MENU! BIG CAT SAW THE DEER GO BEHIND SOME BRUSH AND HE QUICKLY CLOSED THE DISTANCE BETWEEN THEM BY CROUCHING AND PADDING FORWARD SILENTLY.

THEN BEING ABOUT FIFTY FEET FROM THE YEARLING, BIG CAT MADE HIS CHARGE. INSTANTLY, EVERY MUSCLE IN HIS LEAN BODY TIGHTENED AND LAUNCHED HIM FORWARD. THE YEARLING BOUNDED AWAY WITH BIG CAT CLOSE BEHIND. FOLLOWING A DEER TRAIL IS DIFFICULT WHEN RUNNING AT FULL SPEED, THUS THE YOUNG DEER WAS HAVING TROUBLE MANEUVERING AT SUCH A HIGH SPEED.

DEER TRAILS MEANDER THROUGH THE WOODS AROUND TREES AND OVER FALLEN LOGS AND SOMETIMES IN CLOSE QUARTERS. BIG CATS AGILITY WAS HIS ADVANTAGE AS HE GAINED ON THE YEARLING AND JUST AS IT WENT UNDER A HANGING TREE, BIG CAT LAUNCHED FORWARD AND SUNK HIS CLAWS INTO THE HINDQUARTERS OF THE DEER. THE YEARLY DRAGGED HIM ALONG FOR A FEW

JUMPS BUT THE WEIGHT OF THE CAT EXHAUSTED IT AND THE DEER STAGGERED TO A STOP WITH BIG CAT HANGING ON.

WITH ANOTHER LEAP, BIG CAT WAS ON TOP OF THE YEARLING SINKING HIS TEETH INTO THE DEER'S THROAT. WHEN THE YEARLY STOPPED STRUGGLING, BIG CAT CHECKED THE FOREST AREA AROUND HIM FOR SAFETY AND BEGAN TO EAT. STAYING CLOSE BY; HE RETURNED AND FINISHED THE DEER OFF OVER THE NEXT FEW NIGHTS.

CHAPTER 18

NEW COUNTRY AND MORE CLOSE ENCOUNTERS

ONCE MORE THE BIG FREEWAYS GOT IN BIG CAT'S WAY AS HE CROSSED THE COUNTRYSIDE. HE HAD TRAVELED ACROSS A NUMBER OF COUNTRY ROADS AND TWO-LANE HIGHWAYS AND AROUND HOUSING DEVELOPMENTS BUT NOW HE WAS *FENCED IN* BY A SUPER HIGHWAY (FREEWAY) AGAIN.

IN HIS EARLIER SUMMER TRAVELS; BIG CAT CAME UPON A WIDE RIVER AND COULDN'T FIND A SHALLOW SPOT, SO HE SWAM ACROSS JUST AS HE DID WHEN HE WANTED TO GET ACROSS A LONG LAKE. BUT IT WAS WINTER NOW AND HE COULD WALK ACROSS THE ICE TO GET TO ANOTHER FOREST AREA.

AFTER CROSSING THE FREEWAY SAFELY LATE AT NIGHT, BIG CAT MEANDER ACROSS MORE FIELDS AND AROUND FARMS WITH DIFFERENT LIVESTOCK LIKE HORSES, SHEEP, PIGS, CHICKENS AND CATTLE BUT HE FOUND NOTHING EASILY AVAILABLE TO HIM SO HE TRAVELED ON. COMING ONTO A PLANTATION OF LARGE JACK PINES, BIG CAT CROSSED INTO AN OLD FIELD COVERED WITH SHRUB OAK. UNKNOWN TO HIM, A HUNTER SAT IN A TREE NO MORE THAN EIGHTY YARDS FROM HIM AND WAS SHOCKED TO SEE A COUGAR WALK BY HIM. BIG CAT WALKED ACROSS THE FIELD AND WENT INTO SOME THICK BRUSH.

CLIMBING DOWN FROM THE TREE THE HUNTER QUICKLY RAN TO THE ROAD TO SEE IF HE COULD CATCH SITE OF THE COUGAR ON THE ROAD. BIG CAT HAD ALREADY PASSED OVER THE ROAD AND HAD TRAVELED ONTO OTHER HUNTING GROUNDS. NOT FINDING ANY TRACKS AS IT WAS GETTING DARK THE HUNTER

RETURNED THE NEXT DAY AND FOUND BIG CAT'S TRACK CROSSING THE ROAD AND LATER REPORTED IT TO THE DNR.

CATCHING SCENT OF SOME DEER, BIG CAT WAS SCOUTING A CORNFIELD ONE AFTERNOON WHEN SOMEONE ON THE FREEWAY SPOTTED HIM CROSSING A CORNFIELD. BIG CAT PAID NO ATTENTION TO THE TRAFFIC ON THE FREEWAY AS HE WAS USED TO THE RUMBLE. THE DRIVER TURNED HIS CAR AROUND BUT BY THE TIME HE RETURNED BIG CAT HAD DISAPPEARED.

BIG CAT HAD TRAVELED MILES AFTER THAT ENCOUNTER AND HAD JUST ENTERED ANOTHER FOREST AREA WHEN HE CAME FACE TO FACE WITH ANOTHER MALE COUGAR! HUNCHING UP IN A THREATENING POSE THE TWO MOUNTAIN LIONS SNARLED AND SLOWLY CIRCLED EACH OTHER TESTING THE OTHERS CATS ABILITY TO DEFEND ONE SELF. BIG CAT LET OUT A SCREAM OF WARNING AND THE OTHER COUGAR RESPONDED WITH A SIMILAR SCREAM.

JUST LIKE TWO HOUSE CATS IN A FIGHT, BOTH COUGARS CONTINUED TO SCREECH AND HOWL AT ONE ANOTHER IN AN ATTEMPT TO INTIMIDATE THE OTHER. BOTH CATS KNEW BETTER THAN TO FIGHT THE OTHER BECAUSE ANY WOUND WOULD LESSEN THEIR ABILITY TO CATCH GAME AND THEY NEEDED ALL THEIR STRENGTH TO SURVIVE.

THE CIRCLING AND SCREECHING WENT ON FOR ABOUT TEN MINUTES BEFORE THEY BEGAN TO REALIZE THAT NEITHER ONE WAS GOING TO BACK DOWN. SO THEY QUIETED DOWN AND SAT STARING AT ONE ANOTHER WAITING FOR THE OTHER TO MAKE A MOVE. THE OTHER COUGAR WOULD GLANCE AWAY FOR A MOMENT AND THEN LOOK BACK, QUICKLY, TO SEE IF BIG CAT WAS KEEPING HIS DISTANCE. BIG CAT WOULD DO THE SAME AND THIS WENT ON FOR SOME TIME.

FINALLY, THE OTHER COUGAR SLOWLY RAISED ITS FRONT PAW AND TOOK A STEP AWAY FROM BIG CAT PLACING IT DOWN VERY SLOWLY AS IT MOVED AWAY. AFTER WATCHING THE OTHERS ACTIONS FOR A WHILE, BIG CAT MOVED HIMSELF INTO A MORE COMFORTABLE POSITION CURLING HIS TAIL AROUND HIMSELF AS HE WATCHED THE OTHER CAT SLOWLY, SLIP AWAY.

AFTER ABOUT TEN MINUTES OF THIS *SLOW-MOTION GETAWAY* BIG CAT RELAXED AS HE WATCHED THE OTHER CAT DISAPPEAR OUT OF HIS SITE. SNIFFING THE AREA THOROUGHLY, BIG CAT RAISED HIS TAIL AND LEFT HIS SCENT TO PROVE THIS WAS HIS TERRITORY.

ABOUT A HUNDRED YARDS AWAY FROM THE SCUFFLE A HUNTER SAT IN HIS DEER STAND UNABLE TO SEE WHAT WAS HAPPENING AND WAS SHOCKED AND BAFFLED AT HEARING ALL THE SCREECHING AND FRIGHTENING NOISE WHICH SOUNDED TO HIM LIKE A WOMAN SCREAMING AT TIMES! HE DIDN'T KNOW WHAT TO MAKE OF IT?

LATER, WHEN HE WAS PACKING UP TO LEAVE HIS STAND AT DUSK, TWELVE BELGIAN HORSES COME RACING OUT OF THE WOODS INTO THE FIELD NEXT TO HIM. THE FACT THAT SOME OF THE BIGGEST HORSES IN THE WORLD WERE SCARED OUT OF THE WOODS ONLY MADE HIM FEEL MORE FRIGHTEN. SO, THE HUNTER WALKED UP TO THE FARMER HOUSE WHOSE LAND HE WAS HUNTING ON AND TOLD HIM WHAT HAPPENED.

THE FARMER TOLD THE HUNTER THAT HE HAD THE SAME PROBLEM BEFORE WITH HIS HORSES RACING OUT OF THE WOODS AND WHEN HE HAD JUMPED IN HIS TRUCK AND DROVE BACK INTO THE SAME AREA AFTER DARK HIS HEADLIGHTS PICKED UP A LARGE CAT WITH A LONG TAIL THAT DASHED OFF INTO THE CORNFIELD.

BIG CATS ENCOUNTER WITH THE BELGIAN HORSES WAS ONE OF CURIOSITY MORE THAN ANYTHING. HE HADN'T SEEN THE-*LIKES* OF SUCH LARGE CREATURES AND WAS CURIOUS AS TO WHAT THEY WERE AS HE WALKED OUT INTO THEIR SIGHT. THE HORSES WERE JUST AS BAFFLED AND SHOCKED TO SEE SUCH A LARGE CAT AND THEIR INSTINCT TOLD THEM TO RUN.

CHAPTER 19

SEARCHING FOR A PLACE
TO CALL HOME

THANKSGIVING AND CHRISTMAS CAME AND
WENT BUT BIG CAT ONLY NOTICED ODD GLOWING ORNAMENTS IN PEOPLE'S YARDS
AS HE TRAVELED THROUGH MICHIGAN AND ON TO OTHER STATES. LATE ONE NIGHT;
BIG CAT WAS PASSING ALONG THE WOODY SUBURBS OF A CITY AND HE SAW A
HUMAN RIDING DOWN A PATH ON A BICYCLE.

BECAUSE IT WAS SO LATE AT NIGHT, BIG CATS INSTINCT WAS AROUSED. HIS
CURIOSITY AND HIS NATURAL CHASING INSTINCT OVER-TOOK HIM AND HE LOPED
AFTER THE MAN ON THE BICYCLE. THE TWO WEREN'T ALONE, HOWEVER, BECAUSE
A MAN WAS WALKING DOWN THE SAME PATH AHEAD OF THEM.

THE MAN ON THE BICYCLE DIDN'T KNOW THAT BIG CAT WAS RUNNING
AFTER HIM UNTIL HE PASSED THE WALKING MAN AND LOOKED BACK. GLANCING
BACK HE SAW THE COUGAR RUNNING UP TO THE MAN WALKING DOWN THE
PATH BEHIND HIM. PEDALING FASTER IN FEAR THE BICYCLIST CONTINUED ON
GLANCING BACK OFTEN. HE SAW BIG CAT RUN RIGHT UP TO THE MAN THEN
STOP. THE MAN JUMPED BACK IN SURPRISE AND HOLLERED AT THE LARGE CAT.
BIG CAT RAN OFF INTO THE BRUSH AND WATCHED THE MAN WALK AWAY THEN
CONTINUED HIS EXPLORING OF THE AREA STAYING OUT OF SIGHT OF HUMANS.
THE CYCLIST WROTE THAT THIS ALL TOOK PLACE ONLY THREE OR FOUR BLOCKS
FROM DOWNTOWN. (SAVE THE COUGAR.ORG)

COVERING MILES OF FIELDS; SWAMPS AND FORESTS, BIG CAT ENTERED INTO
THE HIAWATHA NATIONAL FOREST WHERE RABBITS, DEER AND OTHER WILD

LIFE WERE PLENTIFUL. AFTER CHASING SOME DEER WITHOUT SUCCESS, BIG CAT CAUGHT THE SCENT OF A FRESH KILL. THE SCENT LED HIM TO A RURAL ROAD WITH A DEAD DOE LYING ON THE SIDE OF THE ROAD KILLED BY A CAR.

AS BIG CAT WALKED UP TO THE DEER A FOX WAS GNAWING ON THE CARCASS AND IT QUICKLY TURNED AND RAN OFF TO SAFETY WHEN IT SAW HIM. BIG CAT SETTLED DOWN TO EAT AND WAS AS ABLE TO GET HIS FILL OF VENISON BEFORE CLEANING HIMSELF UP AND WALKING OFF TO FIND A PLACE TO REST WITHOUT BEING DISTURBED.

AFTER A GOOD DAYS REST IN THE COVER OF SOME JACK PINES, BIG CAT RETURNED TO THE CARCASS. IT WAS EARLY AFTERNOON BUT THE AREA THAT THE DEAD DEER LAY WAS RURAL AND AWAY FROM HEAVY HUMAN TRAFFIC SO HE WASN'T CONCERNED.

AS BIG CAT APPROACHED HE COULD HEAR CROWS CAWING AND THE *SENTENTIAL CROW* STARTED SENDING A WARNING CALL TO THE OTHERS. CROWS ARE VERY INTELLIGENT BIRDS AND THEY ALWAYS HAVE ONE CROW SIT UP HIGH IN A TREE, AS A SENTENTIAL TO SEE ANY DANGER APPROACHING.

ALL THE CROWS QUICKLY TOOK TO THE AIR AND LANDED IN A NEARBY TREE TO CHECK OUT THE REASON FOR THE ALARM. THE CLATTER OF THE CROWS INCREASED WHEN THEY SAW BIG CAT BUT HE PAID NO MIND TO THEM. HE SNIFFED THE CARCASS AND FINDING A FRESH SPOT ON IT HE HUNCHED DOWN TO EAT. THE CROWS, EVENTUALLY, FLEW OFF AND AFTER EATING HIS FILL, BIG CAT RETURNED TO THE JACK PINES TO REST.

ABOUT 8PM THE NEXT EVENING HE WAS RETURNING TO HIS CARCASS TO EAT WHEN CAR LIGHTS LIT UP THE ROAD BY THE DEAD DEER. LIGHTS IN BIG CATS EYES AT NIGHT ALWAYS PUZZLED HIM AS IT SPIKED HIS CURIOSITY AND HE FELT INTRIGUED AND HYPNOTIZED AS THE DAZZLING LIGHTS MADE HIM FORGET THE DANGER.

HOWEVER; IF A LOUD RUMBLING, ROARING SOUND PRECEDED THE BRIGHT LIGHTS HE KNEW DANGER FOLLOWED. THIS TIME THE LIGHTS SEEMED TO FLOAT AT HIM AND HE FELT HIMSELF ENTER INTO A SENSE OF HYPNOTIC STATE AS HE STEPPED OUT ONTO THE ROAD INTO THE LIGHTS.

THE DRIVER WAS SLOWING DOWN AND CAME TO A STOP ABOUT FIFTEEN FEET AWAY FROM BIG CAT. THE DRIVER STARED AT THE BROAD SIDE OF A LARGE CAT AS BIG CAT GAZED AT THE LIGHTS OF THE CAR. AFTER A FEW MOMENTS

BIG CATS SENSED THE DANGER COMING AT HIM AND HE LEAPT OFF THE ROAD AND HID IN SOME TALL SWAMP CATTAILS.

WHEN THE CAR LEFT THE AREA BIG CAT CAME OUT OF THE SWAMP AND RETURNED TO HIS MEAL. GETTING HIS FILL, BIG CAT FOUND A SAFE PLACE TO REST IN A PILE OF BRUSH. THE NEXT DAY WHEN HE RETURNED, BIG CAT SURPRISED AN EAGLE EATING OFF THE DEER AND IT FLEW ACROSS THE ROAD LANDING IN A TREE JUST FAR ENOUGH AWAY TO WATCH THE COUGAR. THE CARCASS WAS MOSTLY BONES AND HIDE AND AFTER BIG CAT ATE FROM THE SCRAPS HE KNEW IT WAS TIME TO MOVE ON AND LOOK FOR OTHER FOOD.

ONE MORNING, BIG CAT SAW SOMETHING MOVING IN THE BRUSH A DISTANCE AWAY FROM HIM WHILE HE WAS SUNNING HIMSELF ON A FALLEN TREE. JUMPING TO THE GROUND AND CROUCHING LOW, HE APPROACHED SLOWLY AND SAW THAT IT WAS A PORCUPINE. THE ANIMAL SAUNTERED ALONG OBLIVIOUS TO ANY DANGER. BIG CAT KNEW FROM EXPERIENCE THAT PORCUPINES WERE TROUBLE BUT HIS HUNGER AND HIS *CATS—CURIOSITY* MADE HIM *THROW CAUTION TO THE WIND!*

WALKING UP TO THE PORCUPINE AS IT WADDLED AWAY, BIG CAT BATTED HIS PAW AT IT. THE PORCUPINE WAS STARTLED AS IT HADN'T SEEN BIG CAT APPROACH HIM BECAUSE OF ITS POOR EYE SIGHT. IT TURNED TOWARDS BIG CAT AND CHATTERED ITS TEETH AT HIM. BIG CAT WASN'T FAZED BY THAT AND REACHED OUT AGAIN WITH HIS RIGHT PAW TO BAT AT IT.

THAT WAS BIG CATS MISTAKE AS THE PORCUPINE SWUNG HIS TAIL, FULL OF QUILLS AT HIS PAW AND BIG CAT QUICKLY WITHDREW IT WHEN HE FELT THE PAIN OF THE QUILLS ENTERING HIS PAW. SITTING AND PULLING AT THE QUILLS WITH HIS TEETH, BIG CAT WATCHED THE PORCUPINE WALK AWAY IN TRIUMPH. HE NEVER DID GET ALL THOSE QUILLS OUT OF HIM!

WINTER FADED INTO SPRING AND BIG CAT HAD CROSSED FROZEN LAKES AND MANY MILES OF FOREST AND FIELDS. DOING HIS BEST TO EVADE MAN AND THEIR FAST TRAVELING ROAD MACHINES, BIG CAT'S TRAVELING BROUGHT HIM INTO A RURAL AREA NEAR A RANCH WITH CHICKENS! HIS MEMORY FLASHED BACK TO THE HEN HOUSE HE HAD INVADED IN THE PAST AND THE FEAST OF TASTY CHICKENS HE HAD EATEN.

DETERMINED AND HUNGRY HE LAY IN THE TALL GRASS WAITING FOR AN OPPORTUNITY TO SNATCH A CHICKEN OR TWO. HOWEVER, IT WAS NOT GOING TO BE EASY BECAUSE THE CHICKENS DIDN'T SEEM TO STRAY FAR FROM THE BUILDINGS AND BIG CAT DIDN'T WANT TO BE SEEN BY THE HUMANS THAT LIVED THERE BY ENTERING THE SHORT, MOWED GRASSY AREA.

CRAWLING ON HIS BELLY, HE SLOWLY CREPT CLOSER TO THE EDGE OF THE GRASS KEEPING HIS BODY AS LOW AS POSSIBLE. NOTHING ELSE AROUND HIM WAS OF ANY IMPORTANCE TO BIG CAT AS HE TOTALLY CONCENTRATED ALL HIS ATTENTION ON THE CHICKENS THAT KEPT LOOKING FOR BUGS IN THE GRASS ACROSS THE LAWN IN FRONT OF HIM. A BLUE JAY FLEW JUST OVER BIG CATS HEAD AND HE BARELY MOVED AN EAR TO LISTEN AS IT PASSED BY.

A HALF HOUR PASSED BY AND THE CHICKENS BEGAN TO SEPARATED AND BIG CAT SAW HIS CHANCE TO GRAB A CHICKEN. WHEN A HEN STRAYED AWAY FROM THE REST OF THE CHICKENS WHILE IT WAS PREOCCUPIED WITH GRASSHOPPERS; BIG CAT CHARGED OUT OF THE TALL GRASS AT IT. THE HEN PANICKED AND STARTED TO RUN WITH ITS WINGS FLAPPING BUT BIG CAT GRABBED IT, TURNED AND RACED BACK TO THE GRASS BEFORE ANYONE NOTICED.

AFTER FINISHING THE CHICKEN, BIG CAT WAITED OUT OF SIGHT HOPING FOR ANOTHER CHICKEN DINNER LATER. HE SETTLED DOWN TO REST UNDER SOME LOW FIR TREE BOUGHS AND WAITED FOR HIS NEXT OPPORTUNITY TO GET ANOTHER CHICKEN AFTER DARK.

THE OWNERS OF THE RANCH LOCKED THE CHICKENS IN A WELL-BUILT CHICKEN HOUSE AND ALTHOUGH BIG CAT WALKED AROUND THE HEN HOUSE SEARCHING FOR AN OPENING MOST OF THE NIGHT HE COULDN'T FIND ANY WAY TO GET INTO THE HEN HOUSE. BIG CAT RETURNED TO THE FIR TREES JUST BEFORE DAYLIGHT. LUCKY FOR BIG CAT THE SNOW HAD MELTED AND HE LEFT NO TRACKS AND THEY DIDN'T HAVE A DOG SO THE OWNERS WERE UNAWARE OF ANY DANGER TO THEIR CHICKENS.

THE ROOSTER STARTED CROWING AT DAYBREAK AND WOKE BIG CAT FROM HIS CAT NAP. THE RANCHER WAS UP EARLY FEEDING THE CHICKENS AND LET THEM OUT OF THEIR PEN. AFTER WAITING TO MAKE SURE ALL WAS CLEAR OF HUMANS, BIG CAT CREPT BACK INTO THE TALL GRASS WHERE HE HAD BEEN SUCCESSFUL BEFORE IN HIS HUNTING,

BIG CAT SET HIS GAZE ON THE ROOSTER THAT MADE THE MISTAKE OF COMING IN HIS DIRECTION. CONFIDENT IN HIS MALE DOMINANCE OVER THE HENS THE ROOSTER STRUTTED ALONG SHOWING OFF THE BEAUTIFUL COLORS OF HIS FEATHERS WITH HIS LONG TAIL FEATHERS BLOWING IN THE WIND. HE DIDN'T EVEN SEE BIG CAT UNTIL IT WAS TOO LATE!

RUNNING, SQUAWKING AND TRYING TO FLEE FROM THE CHARGING COUGAR, THE CHICKEN BARELY RAN A FEW FEET BEFORE BIG CAT'S CLAWS PULLED IT DOWN AND IT WAS OVER. GRABBING THE ROOSTER IN HIS MOUTH BIG CAT RAN OUT INTO THE WEEDS FAR ENOUGH AWAY TO FEEL SAFE AND SETTLED DOWN TO EAT HIS MEAL.

HOWEVER, THIS TIME BIG CAT WASN'T SO LUCKY AS TO GET AWAY WITH THE STOLEN CHICKEN BECAUSE THE NOISE OF THE SQUAWKING ROOSTER HAD CAUGHT

SOME ONES ATTENTION AND THEY CAME OUT TO INVESTIGATE. BIG CAT LOPED AWAY WITH THE ROOSTER IN HIS MOUTH WHEN HE HEARD THEM APPROACHING AND RAN FAR ENOUGH AWAY FROM THEM TO BE ABLE TO FINISH HIS MEAL UNDER SOME LOW PINE BOUGHS. AFTER ALMOST GETTING CAUGHT HE KNEW HE HAD TO CONTINUE ON HIS WAY WITHOUT GOING BACK FOR MORE CHICKENS.

CHAPTER 20

HEADING SOUTH

THE SNOW HAD MELTED AND SMALL FLOWERS WERE STARTING TO SPOUT IN THE FOREST BEDS, AS BIG CATS RESTLESS TRAVELING BOUGHT HIM ACROSS QUEBEC THEN SOUTH INTO THE MORE HUMAN POPULATED AREA OF NEW YORK. HE MADE EVERY ATTEMPT TO STAY AWAY FROM HUMANS AND THEIR CLUSTERED, HOUSING AS HE HUNTED IN THE ADIRONDACK NORTHERN REGIONS OF NEW YORK STATE.

RABBITS WERE PLENTIFUL AND HE WAS ABLE TO SATISFY HIS HUNGER MOST OF THE TIME. ONE TIME HE CAUGHT A GROUSE (PARTRIDGE) SITTING ON A FALLEN TREE BY SURPRISE AS HE CAME AROUND A TREE AND WAS ABLE TO JUMP AND CATCH IT AS IT TRIED TO FLY AWAY. THE GROUSE WAS A SPECIAL TREAT FOR BIG CAT BECAUSE MOST OF THE TIME THEY WERE HARD TO CATCH.

LATER, WHILE CROSSING OVER A HILL COVERED WITH OAKS, BIRCH TREES, POPLAR TREES AND SCATTERED BRUSHY AREAS, HE CAME UPON A POND WITH THE WATER STANDING AROUND THE BASE OF THE TREES WHICH WAS THE AFTER-EFFECT OF BEAVERS DAMMING THE CREEK UP. WALKING ALONG THE EDGE HE LAPPED AT THE WATER AND SEARCHED FOR ANYTHING EDIBLE. THE BEAVERS WERE BUSY COLLECTING BRANCHES FOR THEIR DAM AND HADN'T SEEN BIG CAT ARRIVE.

THE CAT AND THE BEAVER WERE ABOUT FIFTY FEET APART WHEN THE BEAVER DOVE INTO THE WATER MAKING A BIG SPLASH WITH ITS TAIL WHEN IT SPOTTED BIG CAT. WHEN THE BEAVER SURFACED FOR AIR IT SAW BIG CAT CIRCLING AROUND THE POND WAITING FOR HIM TO SURFACED HOPING TO GET

NEAR ENOUGH TO CATCH IT. SO THE BEAVER QUICKLY DOVE UNDER, SWIMMING TO THE ENTRANCE OF ITS UNDERWATER DEN FOR SAFETY. BIG CAT KNEW FROM EXPERIENCE THAT THE BEAVER WOULDN'T COME OUT OF THE DEN FOR SOME TIME, SO HE LEFT SEARCHING FOR ANOTHER MEAL.

THE NEXT MORNING, BIG CAT WAS BACK MORE DETERMINED THAN EVER TO HAVE A BEAVER FOR LUNCH! THIS TIME HE APPROACHED VERY QUIETLY FROM DOWN-WIND IN THAT PERFECT *SLOW-MOVING, STEALTH-LIKE WAY* THAT ONLY A CAT CAN DO!

CREEPING OVER THE RIDGE, HE CAREFULLY CHECKED OUT THE POND BELOW FROM END TO END LOOKING FOR ANY SIGN OF THE BEAVERS. THEN HE SAW THE BEAVER SITTING ON THE EDGE OF THE POND CHEWING ON THE BASE OF A BIG ASPEN TREE WORKING AT DROPPING ANOTHER TREE INTO THE WATER TO ADD TO HIS DAM.

SEEING HIS OPPORTUNITY TO CATCH THE BEAVER OFF GUARD, BIG CAT BEGAN TO CREEP DOWN THE HILL MOVING AROUND FALLEN TREES AND BRANCHES IN HIS WAY AS HE SNUCK UP ON THE BEAVER. BIG CAT MOVED CLOSER AND CLOSER AS THE BEAVER CONTINUED WORKING ON THE TREE UNAWARE OF THE DANGER.

AT THE DISTANCE OF ABOUT SEVENTY FIVE FEET, BIG CAT FROZE WHEN THE BEAVER LOOKED UP. THE LOW–CROUCHING, COUGAR WASN'T SEEN BY THE BEAVER BECAUSE HE WAS PARTIALLY HIDDEN BY A FALLEN TREE, SO THE BEAVER RETURNED TO HIS WORK ON THE TREE. BIG CAT QUICKLY CONTINUED HIS STALKING AND MOVED CLOSER FOR THE KILL.

WHEN BIG CAT WAS TEN TO FIFTEEN FEET AWAY FROM THE BEAVER IT LOOKED UP AND SAW HIM BUT IT WAS TOO LATE! THE BEAVER DOVE FOR THE WATER BUT BIG CAT WAS TOO FAST AND CAUGHT IT JUST AS IT REACHED THE EDGE OF THE POND. IN ONE QUICK MOVEMENT, BIG CAT PULLED IT BACK TO HIM AND BIT THE BEAVER IN THE BACK OF THE NECK AND IT WAS OVER.

AFTER EATING SOME OF THE BEAVER, BIG CAT SCRATCHED LEAVES AND TWIGS ON TOP OF IT AND WALKED OFF TO FIND A SHELTER TO REST. CLIMBING THE RIDGE HE LOOKED FOR A SECURE PLACE TO SLEEP BUT DIDN'T SEE A SUITABLE TREE OR HIDING PLACE TO REST. GLANCING BACK ACROSS THE POND HE SAW A COUPLE FIR TREES WITH LOW HANGING BOUGHS AND WALKED AROUND THE POND TO INVESTIGATE THEM. THE DRY BROWN NEEDLES COVERED THE GROUND UNDER THE BRANCHES AND AFTER THE *"USUAL CIRCLING OF INSPECTION"* THAT CATS LIKE TO DO BEFORE THEY LAY DOWN, BIG CAT SETTLED DOWN FOR A SNOOZE.

SOMETIME LATER A MUFFLED SOUND WOKE BIG CAT FROM HIS SLEEP AND HE STEPPED OUT FROM UNDER THE BOUGHS TO SEE WHAT IT WAS. NOT SEEING ANY THREAT, HE STRETCHED HIS LONG BODY BY STEPPING FORWARD WITH HIS FRONT LEGS AND LOWERED HIS BELLY TO THE GROUND WHICH MADE HIS BACK BOW DOWNWARDS AS HE STRETCHED HIS MUSCLES. THEN, HE STEPPED FORWARD WITH HIS HIND LEGS AND LEANED BACKWARDS WITH HIS WHOLE BODY, HUNCHING HIS BACK UPWARDS AS HE LOOSENED MORE MUSCLES. SUDDENLY, HE HEARD

ANOTHER SOUND THAT SEEMED TO COME FROM THE AREA WHERE HE HAD LEFT THE DEAD BEAVER.

QUICKLY AND QUIETLY, HE TROTTED TOWARDS HIS HIDDEN KILL BUT WHEN HE SAW THAT A COYOTE HAD FOUND IT AND WAS EATING IT; BIG CAT CHARGED THE COYOTE! AT FIRST, THE COYOTE TRIED TO RUN WITH THE BEAVER IN ITS MOUTH BUT IT QUICKLY REALIZED THAT HE BETTER LEAVE THE BEAVER AND RUN FOR HIS LIFE!

WHEN BIG CAT REACHED THE BEAVER CARCASS HE LET THE COYOTE RACE OFF BECAUSE HE HAD HIS PRIZE. THE COYOTE STOPPED AT A DISTANCE THAT HE THOUGHT WAS OUT OF RANGE OF BIG CAT AND LOOKED BACK, THEN TROTTED OFF TO LOOK FOR A SAFER MEAL.

FINISHING UP THE REMAINS OF THE BEAVER, BIG CAT SAT LICKING HIS PAWS AND RUBBING THEM ON HIS FACE UNTIL HE WAS SATISFIED THAT HE WAS CLEAN. ALL THAT REMAINED OF THE BEAVER WAS THE HIDE THAT TRAPPERS CHERISH BUT THIS HIDE WAS IN NO CONDITION TO TRY TO SELL AS IT WAS TORN INTO SCRAPS. AS BIG CAT WALKED OFF ANOTHER BEAVER SPLASHED ITS TAIL IN WARNING AND DOVE UNDER THE WATER DISAPPEARING FROM SIGHT.

IN THE YEARS LEADING UP TO BIG CATS ENTERING THE NORTHEASTERN PART OF NORTH AMERICA THE DNR HAD BEING DOING RESEARCH ON THE POSSIBILITY OF MOUNTAIN LIONS PRESENCE IN THAT PART OF THE COUNTRY. "IN 2003, PARKS CANADA BIOLOGISTS IN FUNDY NATIONAL PARK RETRIEVED TWO HAIR SAMPLES FROM *HAIR SNARES* THAT TESTED POSITIVE FOR COUGAR DNA".

"THE TWO SAMPLES WERE FOUND WITHIN A SHORT DISTANCE OF ONE ANOTHER AND WERE COLLECTED OVER A 3 MONTH PERIOD. SUBSEQUENT TESTING INDICATED THAT THE SAMPLES CAME FROM 2 DIFFERENT ANIMALS. ONE SAMPLE REFLECTED THE SOUTH AMERICAN COUGAR *GENOTYPE*; THE OTHER SAMPLE REFLECTED THE NORTH AMERICAN *GENOTYPE*. THUS, THE COUGAR SAMPLE OF SOUTH AMERICAN GENOTYPE WAS DEFINITIVELY OF CAPTIVE ORIGIN". (COUGARNET. ORG/NORTHEAST.HTML)

ACCORDING TO THE DNA EVIDENCE, BIG CAT WAS OF THE NORTH AMERICAN GENOTYPE SINCE HIS BIRTHPLACE WAS IN THE DAKOTAS. HOWEVER, IT APPEARED THAT OTHER COUGARS HAVE BEEN CAPTURED AND TAKEN FROM THE SOUTH AMERICAS THEN RELEASED IN THE NORTHERN AMERICAS OR CANADA AND HAVE SURVIVED THE TRANSITION AND ADAPTED TO THE NORTHERN CLIMATE.

EVEN "BLACK" PANTHERS (THAT IS PUMAS OR COUGARS) HAVE BEEN SEEN IN THE NORTHEASTERN PART OF THE AMERICAS; MOST LIKELY THEY ESCAPED OR WERE RELEASED FROM CAPTIVITY IN THE NORTHERN PART OF AMERICA AFTER BEING CAPTURED IN THE SOUTHERN HEMISPHERE.

CHAPTER 21

HOME AT LAST

THE ADIRONDACK REGION IN NEW YORK OFFERED A VARIETY OF GAME FOOD FOR BIG CAT. AS HE WALKED ON THE SHORE OF LAKE GEORGE IN UPSTATE NEW YORK, HE CAME UPON A STREAM RUNNING INTO THE LAKE. SEEING FISH WIGGLING IN SHALLOW WATER IS SOMETHING THAT A CAT CAN'T RESIST AND BIG CAT WAS NO EXCEPTION!

AS BIG CAT WALKED UP TO THE STREAM A BROOK TROUT WAS FUTILELY, TRYING TO SWIM TO DEEPER WATER BUT THE SHALLOW WATER BLOCKED HIS ATTEMPTS. QUICKLY, REACHING FOR THE FISH, HE PATTED AT IT AS IT WIGGLED AROUND BUT HE WASN'T ABLE TO GET AHOLD OF IT.

PUTTING ONE FOOT INTO THE SHALLOW CREEK, BIG CAT TRIED TO GET CLOSER BUT THE FISH MANAGED TO GET INTO DEEPER WATER AND OUT OF HIS REACH. SO, STEPPING INTO THE SANDY CREEK BED AND LEAVING HIS FOOT PRINTS IN THE SAND, HE MANEUVERED HIMSELF SO THAT HE WOULD HAVE A BETTER CHANCE OF CATCHING THE TROUT.

SEEING THAT THE FISH HAD ONLY ONE WAY OUT OF HIS DILEMMA INTO DEEPER WATER; BIG CAT WAS MORE DETERMINED THAN EVER TO CATCH THE TROUT AS HE STEPPED INTO THE WATER. STANDING ANKLE DEEP IN THE WATER; BIG CAT WAS READY AS THE TROUT PANICKED, SPLASHING THE WATER VIOLENTLY AS IT TRIED TO ESCAPE PAST HIS FEET.

AS THE TROUT TRIED TO SLIP BY BIG CAT, HE REACHED OUT WITH HIS RIGHT FRONT PAW AND PLUCKED IT OUT OF THE WATER. AFTER HAVING A DELICIOUS MEAL OF TROUT, BIG CAT CLEANED HIMSELF UP AND TRAVELED ON.

ACTING AS A GO-BETWEEN FOR THE DEPARTMENT OF ENVIRONMENTAL PROTECTION (D.E.P.) AND THE GREENWICH POLICE, JOSEPH CASSONE WAS GETTING NUMEROUS CALLS ABOUT COUGAR SIGHTINGS. QUOTE—"IN THE PAST FEW DAYS, EVERY TIME I SIT DOWN TO GET MY OTHER CONSERVATION WORK (DONE), THE PHONE RINGS AND THERE'S BEEN ANOTHER SIGHTING. I CAN'T SAY THIS HASN'T BEEN INTERESTING AND DIFFERENT".

"WE'RE USED TO DEER AND COYOTES BUT NOT MOUNTAIN LIONS. THE MOST RECENT SIGHTING WAS REPORTED ON WEDNESDAY AT PARTRIDGE HOLLOW LANE NEAR THE BORDER WITH NORTH CASTLE, N. Y . . ." (CASE REPORT/ WPU#100948 /EXAMINER;K.HYNES).

STAYING IN THE LESS POPULATED, WOODED AREA; BIG CAT MOVED IN A SOUTHERLY DIRECTION TRAVELING INTO THE NORTHEAST SECTION OF GREENWICH, CONNECTICUT. HE WAS PASSING BY PARTRIDGE HOLLOW LANE NEAR GREENWICH WHEN; ALL OF A SUDDEN TWO DOGS STARTED BARKING A SHORT DISTANCE AWAY.

STOPPING TO LISTEN; BIG CAT REALIZED THAT THE DOGS WERE "HOT ON HIS TRAIL". BOUNDING OFF; HE NOTICED A WOMAN AND HER DOG WALKING DOWN A PATH IN FRONT OF HIM BUT QUICKLY PASSED BY THEM AS HE RUN AWAY FROM THE PURSUING DOGS. THE YAPPING OF THE HOUNDS SOUNDED DIFFERENT TO HIM THEN THE HOUNDS THAT HAD CHASED HIM IN THE PAST BUT HE KNEW HE NEEDED TO GET OUT OF THE AREA, REGARDLESS OF WHAT KIND OF DOGS THEY WERE.

SEEING A FENCE LINE AHEAD OF HIM HE HEADED THAT WAY AND LEAPED OVER IT AND RAN ON THROUGH THE TREES. AFTER RUNNING FOR AWHILE THROUGH THE WOODS, HE NOTICED THAT THE BARKING OF THE DOGS WAS LETTING UP SO HE SLOWED DOWN AND RELAXED WHEN HE HEARD THE BARKING STOP. THE WOMAN AND HER DOG, LATER COMMENTED THAT SHE HAD SEEN TWO BASSET HOUNDS CHASING A COUGAR.

THE MONTH OF MAY WAS ALMOST OVER AND BIG CAT'S COAT WAS BEGINNING TO THIN OUT AS THE DAYS GREW LONGER AND THE NIGHTS WARMER. WITH A LESS DENSE FUR COAT, HE FELT COOLER; HOWEVER IT HAPPENED SO GRADUAL HE WASN'T AWARE OF THE CHANGE. TRAVELING SOUTH AND ENTERING INTO THE MORE POPULATED AREAS OF THE EASTERN COAST, HE FOUND IT MORE AND MORE DIFFICULT TO FIND FOOD. GREY SQUIRRELS WERE PLENTIFUL BUT HARD

TO CATCH. RABBITS WERE FEW AND WHEN HE DID FIND THEM THEY USUALLY LIVED CLOSE TO OR UNDER ONE OF THE HUMANS' DWELLINGS.

SO BIG CAT COVERED A LOT OF GROUND EVERY NIGHT LOOKING FOR HIS NEXT MEAL. OCCASIONALLY, HE WOULD CATCH A MOUSE TO EAT AND GROUND SQUIRRELS WERE A TASTY TREAT WHEN HE FOUND THEM BUT THEY WERE ONLY AN APPETIZER FOR HIM.

ONE EVENING HE CAUGHT THE SCENT OF A DEER AND FOLLOWED ITS TRAIL. THE TRAIL CROSSED A LITTLE OPENING THEN INTO A GROUP OF PINE TREES WHERE THE PRESENCE OF OTHER DEER SCENTS DISTRACTED HIM. THE BOUGHS OF THE PINE TREES HUNG DOWN AND BLOCKED HIS VIEW AS HE SEARCHED AROUND FOR THE SCENT OF THE DEER HE WAS TRAILING.

FINALLY, FINDING THE FRESH TRAIL OF HIS DEER AFTER SEARCHING FOR SOME TIME THROUGH THE PINES; BIG CAT CONTINUED AFTER THE DEER. COMING OUT OF THE PLANTATION, BIG CAT FOLLOWED THE TRAIL OF THE DEER AS IT WENT OVER A HILL AND DOWN A RAVINE. BECAUSE IT WAS A DARK NIGHT; BIG CAT HAD TO USE HIS NOSE MORE THEN HIS EYES TO STAY ON THE TRAIL OF THE DEER.

BRUSH WAS ALSO A PROBLEM AS HE TRAVELED THROUGH THE THICK WOODS BUT HIS WHISKERS ALERTED HIM WHEN ANY SMALL BRANCHES OR TWIGS WERE IN THE WAY. THE SCENT OF THE DEER BEGAN TO GET FRESHER AND BIG CAT KNEW THAT THE DEER WASN'T FAR AHEAD. SLOWING DOWN HIS STALKING; HE APPROACHED CAREFULLY STOPPING AND LISTENING OFTEN.

SUDDENLY, A DOE JUMPED UP IN FRONT OF HIM AND THE CHASE BEGAN. RACING OFF THROUGH THE WOODS BOTH CAT AND DEER WEAVED BACK AND FORTH THROUGH THE TREES. GAINING ON THE DEER WAS DIFFICULT FOR BIG CAT BECAUSE OF THE TREES AND THE WINDING TRAIL.

BURSTING OUT OF THE WOODS ONTO THE ROAD, THE DOE WAS ALMOST HIT BY A PASSING CAR DRIVING DOWN THE ROAD THAT SHE WAS RACING ACROSS. BIG CAT RACED RIGHT BEHIND HER AND CLEARED THE ROAD IN JUST ENOUGH TIME SO THAT HE WASN'T HIT BY THE CAR AS HE PURSED THE DEER.

THE MAN DRIVING THE CAR HAD TO HIT THE BRAKES ABRUPTLY IN ORDER NOT TO HIT THE FLEEING ANIMALS AS THEY SPRINTED ACROSS THE ROAD IN FRONT OF HIM. WITH THE INTERFERENCE OF THE CAR, THE DOE WAS ABLE TO GET FAR ENOUGH AHEAD OF BIG CAT THAT HE LOST HER TRAIL AND WHEN HE

DID FIND IT, HE SAW THAT SHE HAD GONE NEAR A HOUSING DISTRICT THAT WASN'T SAFE FOR HIM TO ENTER. REALIZING THAT HE HAD BETTER LOOK FOR ANOTHER MEAL; BIG CAT STARTED SEARCHING ON AN EMPTY STOMACH.

IT WAS THE NOW JUNE 2011 AND BIG CAT FOUND HIMSELF NEAR THE OCEAN WITHOUT MANY OPTIONS OF ESCAPING THE PEOPLE AND TRAFFIC. WHEREVER HE TURNED, HE FOUND BUSY ROADWAYS WITH HOUSES AND PEOPLE EVERYWHERE! WHEN HE TRIED TO FIND SHELTER IN THE TREES HE WOULD COME OUT ONTO SOME HUMANS BACK YARD OR THEY WOULD BE WALKING ON TRAILS IN THE WOODS AND SEE HIM.

EVEN AT NIGHT IT SEEMED THAT HE COULDN'T HUNT FOR A MEAL WITHOUT COMING ACROSS SOME HUMAN WALKING A TRAIL OR A CAR PASSING BY HIM. IF HE DID ESCAPE NOTICE FROM HUMANS, THEN A DOG WOULD SCENT HIM AND START BARKING AND DRIVE HIM OFF!

WHILE HE WAS SEARCHING FOR FOOD, HE WAS FORTUNATE ENOUGH TO COME UPON A DEER KILLED BY A CAR LYING IN THE BOTTOM OF A RAVINE OUT OF SIGHT. HE STAYED IN THE AREA AND FEED OFF THE DEER FOR A FEW DAYS BECAUSE HE WAS UNDETECTED THERE BY HUMANS.

HOWEVER, FINDING SHELTER TO ESCAPE HUMAN DISCOVERY WAS DIFFICULT. ON THE FIRST DAY AFTER FEEDING ON THE DEER, BIG CAT HAD JUST SETTLED DOWN UNDER SOME LOW-HANGING PINE BOUGHS WHEN TWO HUMANS CAME WALKING DOWN A *HARDLY USED* TRAIL AND SAW HIM.

RACING OFF; HE FOUND ANOTHER TEMPORARY SHELTER IN SOME THICK BRUSH. ON THE SECOND DAY AFTER EATING FROM THE DEER THE PREVIOUS NIGHT, HE WAS SEEKING ANOTHER SHELTER TO REST WHEN HE SAW SOME HUMAN IN THEIR BACKYARD AS HE PASSED BY BEFORE FINDING A PLACE TO CURL UP AND REST.

ON SUNDAY, JUNE 9TH, 2011 BIG CAT WAS SEEN BY THE BRUNSWICK PREP SCHOOL IN THE GREENWICH AREA BY FACULTY MEMBERS OF THE SCHOOL AS HE PASSED BY. AFTER ABOUT A WEEK OF FEEDING OFF THE ROAD KILL, HE STARTED LOOKING FOR BETTER HUNTING GROUNDS. THE DEER REMAINS WERE GONE AND WITH OTHER SCAVENGERS LIKE, FOXES, COYOTES, EAGLES AND CROWS WORKING ON IT, BIG CAT LEFT THE REMAINS OF THE KILL AND MOVED ON.

TRAVELING SOUTH ALONG THE BAY AREA DIDN'T WORK FOR BIG CAT AS HE DISCOVERED THERE WERE FAR TOO MANY HOUSES AND VERY LITTLE WOODED

AREAS TO HUNT AND HIDE IN. CHANGING HIS COURSE; BIG CAT ENDED UP TRAVELED IN A NORTHERLY DIRECTION ALONG THE SHORELINE OF LAKE MICHIGAN WHERE HE FOUND AN OCCASIONAL CRAB OR DEAD FISH.

QUITE OFTEN, HE WOULD HAVE TO DUCK OUT OF SIGHT AND SOMETIMES TRAVEL A LITTLE INLAND TO GET AROUND HUMAN DWELLING PLACES AS HE HEADED NORTH ALONG THE COASTLINE. EXPLORING THE ROCKY SHORELINE; HE WOULD SEE BOATS DRIFT BY IN THE BAY AND WOULD STAND AND WATCH THEM PASS BY. MOST WOULDN'T EVEN NOTICE BIG CAT WATCHING THEM ALONG THE SHORELINE AS THEY SAILED BY.

FINDING A CAVE HE EXPLORED THE TUNNEL AS IT CAREENED BACK UNDER THE BANK. THE FLOOR OF THE CAVE WAS SANDY WITH A LITTLE WATER STANDING IN IT AND BIG CAT WAS ABLE TO FIND SCRAPS OF FISH AND OTHER THINGS TO EAT AS HE EXPLORED THE CAVE. FINDING A RESTING PLACE IN THE CAVE; BIG CAT FELT A LITTLE LESS ANXIOUS BEING OUT OF THE ROAR OF THE TRAFFIC AND CONSTANT HUMAN PRESENCE.

JUNE 11TH, 2011 WAS JUST ANOTHER DAY OF SURVIVAL FOR BIG CAT AS HE TRIED TO AVOID HUMANS AND FIND FOOD. HE HAD TRAVELED UP THE COASTLINE AND WAS NEAR MILFORD, CONNECTICUT THAT EVENING WHEN HE CAME UPON A MAJOR ROADWAY BLOCKING HIS WAY.

WALKING UP AND DOWN THE FENCE LINE THAT RAN ALONG THE ROADWAY, BIG CAT COULDN'T DECIDE WHERE THE SAFEST ROUTE WOULD BE TO CROSS-OVER TO THE OTHER SIDE. SEEING AN OPEN GRASSY AREA EXPANDING BEFORE THE ROADWAY, HE JUMPED THE FENCE AND TRAVELED DOWN THE GRASSY EMBANKMENT TOWARDS THE ROAD.

TRAFFIC WAS BUSY ON THE ROAD AS HE WAITED TO CROSS OVER AND THE ROAR OF THE CARS AND THEIR CLOSE ENCOUNTERS MADE HIM NERVOUS. SEEING AN OPENING HE DASHED ACROSS THE ROAD IN HOPES OF GETTING AWAY FROM ALL THE TRAFFIC. HOWEVER; HE DIDN'T REALIZE THE APPROACHING SUV WAS TRAVELING AS FAST AS IT WAS TOWARDS HIM. FOR A SPLIT-SECOND HE SAW A BLUR COMING AT HIM . . . THEN ALL WET BLACK!

As the Blackness lifted; Big Cat discovered that he was back in the Black Hills, again!

He found it unbelievable that he was suddenly, back home where he grew up.

Slowly, he began to realize that it was true!

The familiar scents of his homeland filled his nostrils.

The high bluffs and the lack of trees, verified the fact that all this was REAL!

After a few more minutes of studying his natural surroundings, Big Cat looked into the cave in front of him and was delighted to see his mother, sister and brother lying together in front of him—*Alive!*

Taking a second look he had to accept the fact that his whole family was alive and <u>really</u>, right in front of him.

As he skeptically, approached his family, he suddenly realized that *he too* was a *kitten*—again! Just like his brother and sister in front of him!

Overcome with joy and contentment, Big Cat snuggled in beside his siblings and began to purr as his mother licked his head . . .

THE END